STAMPED

(For Kids)

Racism, Antiracism, and You

STAMPED

(For Kids)

Racism, Antiracism, and You

Adapted by
SONJA CHERRY-PAUL
from *Stamped: Racism, Antiracism, and You* by
JASON REYNOLDS,
a Remix of *Stamped from the Beginning* by
IBRAM X. KENDI

With art by RACHELLE BAKER

LITTLE, BROWN AND COMPANY
New York   Boston

Adapted from *Stamped: Racism, Antiracism, and You (A Remix of the National Book Award–winning Stamped from the Beginning)*, published in hardcover in March 2020 by Little, Brown and Company.

Text copyright © 2021 by Ibram X. Kendi and Jason Reynolds
Illustrations copyright © 2021 by Rachelle Baker

Cover art copyright © 2021 by Rachelle Baker
Cover design by Karina Granda
Cover copyright © 2021 by Hachette Book Group, Inc.

Little, Brown and Company
Hachette Book Group
1290 Avenue of the Americas, New York, NY 10104
Visit us at LBYR.com

First Edition: May 2021

Little, Brown and Company is a division of Hachette Book Group, Inc.
The Little, Brown name and logo are trademarks of Hachette Book Group, Inc.

The publisher is not responsible for websites (or their content) that are not owned by the publisher.

Library of Congress Cataloging-in-Publication Data
Names: Cherry-Paul, Sonja, author, adapter. | Kendi, Ibram X., author. | Reynolds, Jason, author. | Baker, Rachelle, illustrator.
Title: Stamped (for kids) : racism, antiracism, and you / adapted by Sonja Cherry-Paul, from "Stamped: Racism, Antiracism, and You" by Jason Reynolds, a remix of "Stamped from the Beginning" by Ibram X. Kendi ; with art by Rachelle Baker.
Other titles: Racism, antiracism, and you
Description: First edition. | New York : Little, Brown and Company, 2021. | Adapted from "Stamped: Racism, Antiracism, and You (A Remix of the National Book Award–winning "Stamped from the Beginning"), published in hardcover in March 2020 by Little, Brown and Company. | Audience: Ages 6–10 | Summary: "A chapter book adaptation of Stamped: Racism, Antiracism, and You: A Remix of the National Book Award-winning "Stamped from the Beginning." —Provided by publisher.
Identifiers: LCCN 2021001030 | ISBN 9780316167581 (hardcover) | ISBN 9780316167383 (ebook) | ISBN 9780316165594 (ebook other)
Subjects: LCSH: African Americans—History—Juvenile literature. | Racism—United States—History—Juvenile literature. | United States—Race relations—History—Juvenile literature.
Classification: LCC E185 .C5125 2021 | DDC 305.800973—dc23
LC record available at https://lccn.loc.gov/2021001030

ISBNs: 978-0-316-16758-1 (hardcover), 978-0-316-16738-3 (ebook)

Printed in the United States of America

LSC-C

Printing 1, 2021

To January Hartwell,
my great-great-great-grandfather
—JR

To the lives they said don't matter
—IXK

To Big Ma and Bully for all you've sowed
—SCP

To Bridgette, my mom, always
—RB

CONTENTS

TALKING ABOUT RACE

Dear Reader,

You may be wondering, *What is this book, exactly?* Because you're used to reading fictional stories. Fairy tales, fantasies about heroes and monsters, or sleepy stories about funny-talking times way before any of you were born. You've probably read several nonfiction books, too. Books about the solar system, cool animals like wolverines, historical events such as the Revolutionary War, and biographies of trailblazers like Harriet Tubman, Rosa Parks, or Martin Luther King Jr. When you've read books about people and events from the past, you may have thought, *What does this have to do with my life today?* Well, this book includes the past *and* is directly connected to our lives as we live them right this minute.

As you read this book, you'll come across lots of people. You may already know about some of them, but this book may make you think about them in a whole new way. In fact, you may even look at your own life differently.

See, this is a present book. Not like a birthday present book, but like an everyday present book. Or maybe just an everyday book. A book about the here and now. A book that can help you understand, for example, what the Black Lives Matter movement today is all about. A book that can help you to better understand where we are in this moment as Americans and how we got here—especially when it comes to race.

Uh-oh. The R-word. You may have been told not to talk about race. Or been made to feel like you can't, as if it's some kind of bad word. But it's not. It shouldn't be. It *can't* be. So let's all just take a deep breath. Inhale. Hold it. Exhale and breathe out:

R A C E

See? Not so bad. We'll continue to take time to pause—to breathe and feel—and unpause as you read, think, and talk about race. Besides, talking about race is one of the most important skills you can learn. Think about the coolest thing you can do. Being able to talk about race is that, times two. And three times as important. Here's why:

Until we learn to talk about race, the poison of racism won't go away.

———◆◆◆———

As you read and think about race, also think about rope. Sometimes rope can be a lifeline. It helps climbers safely move upward and protects them from falling. Sometimes rope can be a weapon. It can be used to control and cause harm. Rope can also join people and things together in powerful ways. Like jumping double Dutch brings all your friends together in the summer. Or like a swing connected to a play set or the branch of a tree that takes you sky-high.

Rope can be used to tie, pull, hold, and lift.

How do people become tied to racist and antiracist ideas? Who are the people pulling at each end? How do racist ideas hold people down? How do antiracist ideas lift people up?

How did things get so tangled in the first place? And who are the people working to unravel this mess?

As you hold on to the image of rope, also keep three words in mind. Three words to describe the people we'll be exploring and the ideas they're tied to:

SEGREGATIONIST
ASSIMILATIONIST
ANTIRACIST

There are serious definitions to these things, but... I'm going to give you mine.

Segregationists are haters. Like, *real* haters. People who hate you for not being like them.

Assimilationists are people who like you *only* if you act like them.

And then there are antiracists. They love you because you are you.

These aren't just words we'll be using to describe the people in this book. Remember, this is more than just a past book. It's a present book. An everyday book. So these are the words we'll be using to describe who you, and me, and all of us are...every day.

Along the way you'll notice that people aren't always just one way. They can believe in and express any one of those three ideas—sometimes all in the same sentence. Also, and most important, people can change.

I repeat:

PEOPLE CAN CHANGE.

Since the beginning of the United States of America, there have been different ideas about what freedom means and who freedom is for. These differing ideas have always been connected to race. This book is meant to take you on a race journey from then to now, with some people you just may think of as new heroes. Antiracists, who help us see ourselves. Who love you because you are you.

·One last thing: something you'll see in this book is that all stories have points of view. And in these pages, you'll hear *my* voice, taking you on this journey. But I want to be clear: This is not a book of my opinions. This is a book about America, and about you. This book is full of *truth*. It's packed with the absolutely true *facts* of the choices people made over hundreds of years

to get us to where we are today. The choices people are still making.

So remember as you read that you are part of writing the next chapter. The choices you make, the words you use, the way you look at yourself and those around you—they all matter. *You* matter. I hope you believe that the world can be good, that things can change, and that knowing this history can help us move toward a better, more honest future. Every day.

I

A Great Big Lie
1415–1619

OKAY, WHERE SHOULD WE START? WE MIGHT AS WELL just jump in and begin with the first hater to make racist ideas popular. It was way, way, *wayyyyyy* back in 1415, when Europeans were busy conquering a bunch of countries. And when they'd conquer a place, they'd capture and enslave people who already lived there like picking up souvenirs on vacation.

Back then, slavery had nothing to do with skin color. Didn't matter what you looked like, it just mattered that you were conquered. Until this hater, a man named Gomes Eanes de Zurara, made new ideas about slavery famous. New ideas that *did* connect slavery to skin color. As well as the idea of making a lot of money by trading enslaved people. How did Zurara do this?

Through storytelling.

Let's PAUSE

Words matter. Stories matter. Lies matter. They can influence the way we think, what we believe, and how we act. As we continue, pay attention to the way words, stories, and lies do just that—how they influence what we think about people and race...and how we act.

Let's UNPAUSE

Zurara wrote a book, a biography of the life and slave trading of his boss, Prince Henry of Portugal. Zurara wasn't the one *actually* enslaving or physically attacking Africans. As a matter of fact, he was on the sidelines. But he wrote the story, so he made the rules. And he used this story—his messed-up fairy tale—to make Prince Henry seem like some kind of good guy. Like his passion for kidnapping and enslaving Africans was something noble instead of something evil.

Zurara spoke about owning humans as if they were cool pairs of sneakers, even though he described Africans as "savage animals" that needed training, which is *definitely* not the way we talk about sneakers. So maybe he viewed them as dress shoes. Shiny black things that had to be worn and worn and worn until they break and soften and become comfortable on your feet. And, what's worse, he claimed that enslaving Africans was a mission from God. God? Can you believe that? And that it was the Europeans' duty to civilize and tame them—to teach them Christianity in order to save their wretched souls. Over time, these racist lies would begin to convince even some African people that they weren't as good as White people.

Zurara was the first person to write about and defend *Black* human ownership, and his book, which was a hit, planted false, anti-Black, racist ideas in a lot of

Europeans' minds. It didn't take long for those ideas to seep in and stick.

After Zurara's ridiculous lie, other Europeans followed in his racist footsteps to spread their own racist ideas to justify slavery. Copycats. Some decided that Africans were inferior, less human, and were Black simply because the weather in Africa is hot, and that if they lived in colder temperatures, they could become White. Ridiculous! One English writer said Blackness was a curse by God. Also ridiculous! More nonsense ideas were that because Africans were "cursed," they *needed* to be enslaved in order for that curse to be lifted. And that the relationship between enslaved people and their enslavers was kind and loving—more like children and their parents. Definitely RIDICULOUS! These ideas were attempts to paint a fake picture about the terrible experience for human beings who were forced into slavery, all so that White enslavers felt better about enslaving Black people.

And when Europeans took over the land that they'd later call America, they brought all of these ridiculous, fool-headed, harebrained ideas with them.

2

Stolen Land, Stolen Lives
1619–1688

IN 1619, THE FIRST SHIP CARRYING ENSLAVED AFRICAN people arrived in the newly colonized America. America welcomed slavery with open arms and used it to build this new country.

Years passed. More and more Europeans arrived, too, running away from haters of their own and seeking freedoms and opportunities. Some of these new arrivals were missionaries, religious folks who wanted to spread their religion, including Puritan ministers who followed strict religious rules. When they came to America, they set up churches and schools to teach their way of thinking: that they were better than any-one who wasn't a Puritan, and *way* better than Native American and African people. They taught those ideas in their churches and schools, which, along with Zu-rara's ideas and others, helped justify slavery for a long, long time—because it was tied to church and school, which are basically the bacon and eggs of the country. Or maybe the bread and cheese. The meat and potatoes? You get the point.

Americans acted like they were playing one of those video games where you have to build a world. Except that's racist. Native Americans had already built a world. But a social network of farmers and missionaries forcefully took over this Native world, by taking over their land.

And what were they doing on that land? Planting and harvesting tobacco. Tobacco's not a big plant, but it can bring in big money. Rich Europeans would pay top dollar for tobacco to smoke and sniff. But if tobacco was *really* going to bring in big, BIG money and become the natural resource used to power the country, then farm-ers would need more *human* resources to grow it.

See where this is going? Slavery.

But remember, America was full of church folk and dirt folk. And the new enslaved Africans would cause a bit of conflict between the two. For the planters, slavery meant they didn't have to pay people to work the fields, so labor by those who were enslaved made them lots of money. For the missionaries, slavery meant new souls to convert to their brand of Christianity. Basically, planters wanted to grow profits, while missionaries wanted to grow their church.

No one cared what the enslaved Africans wanted, but I'm willing to bet they didn't want the religion of their enslavers. And they definitely didn't want to be enslaved.

Some of the enslavers resisted the missionaries' pressure to convert enslaved Africans. They didn't care as much about "saving souls" as they cared about saving their crops and making more money. Many enslavers even worried that if enslaved people had the same religion as them, then they could no longer enslave them. So they made up racist excuses for why enslaved Africans couldn't be converted, like that Africans were wild and inhuman. Unworthy of love from anyone. Even from God.

3

People Aren't Property
1688–1772

MANY OTHER EUROPEANS CONTINUED ZURARA'S tradition of harmful writings about Africans—using words to influence people's beliefs and actions. A British minister named Richard Baxter said slavery *helped* African people and that there were Africans who *wanted* to be enslaved so that they could be baptized. An English philosopher named John Locke said only White people had pure and perfect minds. Italian philosopher Lucilio Vanini said Africans were pretty much a different species from White people. Basically, a whole bunch of people were saying a whole bunch of baloney about Africans just to justify slavery.

[Let's **PAUSE**]

I know we've been going on and on about the people working to justify slavery, but it's important (very important) to note that there were also people all along the way who fought against racist ideas with abolitionist ideas. Ideas about freedom.

Members of one Christian group circulated an antislavery petition that compared cruelty due to skin color to cruelty due to religion. Both oppressions were wrong. This petition in 1688 was the first piece of anti-racist writing among European colonizers in America.

But racist ideas, like tangled rope, are not easy to unravel.

> Think about the way rope connects things. Now think about what racist ideas have been connected to so far: Skin color. Money. Religion. Land.

[Let's UNPAUSE]

In America, rich White landowners worried that poor White people who didn't own land would band together with Native Americans and enslaved Africans to try to make their own lives better. To make sure they'd get more land, more money, more power, the landowners decided they needed poor Whites—*all* Whites, in fact—to feel like they were on the same side, that they were special. How'd they do this? By deciding that all White people would have *privilege*—benefits and protections just for being White—no matter how little or how much money they had. All White people would be thought of and treated as special, better than all non-Whites, and would now have absolute power to punish and abuse any African person.

But with so many more enslaved people working the fields for free, enslavers feared an uprising. A revolt. So they created a bunch of racist rules, such as laws keeping Black people from marrying White people, keeping Black people from going where they wanted when they wanted, and keeping Black people from being in positions of power.

But the main rule, the one that made slavery stick? Treating enslaved people like property. A thing you purchase and own. Like horses and hogs. Not as humans. And certainly not humans with intelligence.

BLACK GIRL POET

Phillis Wheatley was #BlackGirlMagic before there was ever such a thing as hashtags. She joined words and lines to create verses that rhymed—a poet at a time when it was made basically impossible

for a Black girl to be one. She became the first African American woman to publish a book.

As a young girl, Wheatley had been captured and brought to America. She was purchased by the Wheatley family, who homeschooled her. By eleven, she'd written her first poem. By twelve, she could read Greek and Latin classics, English literature, and the Bible. By fourteen, she published her first poem. By nineteen, she had written so many poems, she began gathering them into a collection. A book.

Wheatley disrupted the belief that Black people weren't intelligent by turning that racist idea upside down. She had intelligence and creativity that White people just couldn't believe!

A lot of White people accepted the ridiculous, racist idea that enslaved Black people couldn't possibly be smart. Then a doctor who was against slavery came along and said that Phillis Wheatley was proof that

Black people weren't born savages, but were *made* inhuman by slavery. Uh-oh! Do you see the problem here? He's still saying that Black people are inhuman! Which is racist. And it's assimilationist to ignore the smarts and arts of enslaved Africans, to say that a Black person had to be like Wheatley (who was taught by and like White people) in order to be considered smart.

Remember, a racist idea is any idea that suggests something is wrong or right, superior or inferior, better or worse, about a racial group. An antiracist idea is any idea that suggests that racial groups are equal.

Which brings us back to Wheatley: being a Black girl poet, during a time when poetry was only for and by rich White people, meant no one would publish her book. At least, no one in America.

The British published Wheatley's work. And they used her work—her intelligence—as a way to look down on American slavery. With slavery done away with in Britain, and with Britain in control of America, it made sense that the British government might soon outlaw slavery in their American colonies.

But slavery was the American cash machine. It provided free labor to produce resources that would help America grow, which provided money money money for White Americans. And in order for White Americans to feel comfortable with continuing slavery, they had to break free of Britain once and for all.

4

Flawed Founding Fathers
1776–1787

Learning about the history of racism means discovering that some people, even some who you may have considered heroes, were deeply flawed individuals who had racist thoughts and did racist things. It can feel crushing. *Oof.* But hey, it's not easy being a truth seeker.

But here's the thing. Knowing the truth of the past helps you understand the truth of today, and to make different choices. To stamp out racist ideas and embrace antiracist ones.

Which brings us to Thomas Jefferson.

In 1776 America was doubling down on owning people, but didn't want to be owned by Great Britain. Talk about a contradiction. And, speaking of contradiction, no one was more wishy-washy than Thomas Jefferson. You've probably heard of Jefferson. He's the guy who wrote the Declaration of Independence, America's freedom document, which stated that "all men are created equal." But were enslaved people seen as men? And what about women? Was he talking about freedom for everyone or just for America from England? And what did it mean that antiracist portions of the Declaration, like where Jefferson called slavery a "cruel war against human nature," were edited out of the final document?

It's confusing enough to make your head spin! In fact, when it came to Black people, Jefferson's thoughts were often confusing. The man who wrote America's freedom document also owned more than six hundred enslaved people throughout his life, and wrote a book in which he said that Black people were unequal to White people. His actions and ideas were racist. In fact, most of the Founding Fathers—the leaders who determined how America, as a country, would be run—enslaved people and expressed racist ideas even as they fought for their own freedom from Britain.

———◆•◆———

Eventually, after years of fighting against the British, America did break free of their control. It came out of the Revolutionary War needing a stronger government, so the Founders wrote a new constitution. And guess what was baked right into this constitution? Racist ideas.

Here's one example. The Founding Fathers tried to figure out how much power each state would have in the government. We call this representation.

They decided that the number of people representing a state would be based in part on how many people lived in that state. Bigger states with more people liked this idea because they wanted more of a say in the government. Imagine a class with more students being able to pick what the cafeteria serves for lunch. You want crinkle-cut fries, but the bigger class says, nope, we're eating curly! That would be pretty scary, right? Well, the same fear was felt by smaller states because they felt their needs would be ignored.

And what about the states in the South that had more enslaved people than states in the North? If enslaved people were counted as people, the southern states would certainly be set up to have a bigger voice in government. The northern states saw right through this. Since enslaved people were "owned" and treated as property, why should they suddenly count as human beings?

The Founding Fathers decided to compromise. This agreement involved...a fraction. Each enslaved person would NOT count as a complete, whole human being. Instead they'd count as three-fifths of a person. So just to do the math, five enslaved people would equal three White people.

Southern states agreed because they would still get a little more representation and power in the government. Northern states agreed because southern states wouldn't get *as much* power as they might have if enslaved people counted as...people, instead of fractions. Assimilationists and segregationists were satisfied because it fit right into the argument that Black people were not fully human. (Crinkle and curly...and racism for all!)

Math was used as a weapon against Black people. And this agreement allowed slavery and racist ideas to be stamped permanently into the Constitution of America.

[Let's
PAUSE]

While there were people working to justify slavery, there were people who fought against it. Racist voices overpowered antiracist ones. Yet Black people have always resisted and fought against racist ideas. Hold on to this.

[Let's
UNPAUSE]

5

Fighting Back
1790–1804

ALL OVER THE SOUTH, ENSLAVED PEOPLE RAN AWAY to free states whenever they could.

Some abolitionists, who objected to slavery, urged Black Americans who escaped slavery to live and behave in ways that would make White people accept them. For example, they said Black people should go to church regularly, learn to speak "proper" English, learn trades, and get married, all in order to prove to White people that all the stereotypes about Black people were wrong.

Black people were encouraged not to be themselves, but to change in order to fit into White people's ideas of what it means to be civilized and human. This is racist. Because what these abolitionists were *really* saying is that Black people needed to make themselves small, unthreatening, quiet, and meek, and to be followers, just to be left alone by White people. This is the basis of assimilationist thought—that Black people should behave in ways that make White people comfortable with their existence.

Remember this.

[Let's
UNPAUSE]

Enslaved people wanted freedom and were willing to risk their lives for it. And the fight for freedom wasn't happening just in America. It was happening in other countries, too. Like Haiti.

France, like England, is a European country that conquered other nations around the world. Haiti was one of them. In 1791, Black people resisted. Close to half a million enslaved Africans in Haiti rose up and fought against the French. And they *won*! And because of that victory, Haiti—not the United States—would become a symbol of freedom. And that was scary to all American enslavers because they knew the Haitian Revolution would inspire enslaved people in America to fight back, too.

Inspired by the Haitian Revolution, enslaved people in the United States continued to plan ways to escape or revolt. For freedom. Allies were recruited. They were White, Native American,

Methodists, Quakers. Antiracists of any color and religion were necessary in the struggle for freedom.

They were more important than assimilationists— even Black assimilationists.

For example, several thousand enslaved people and allies planned what would have been the largest slave revolt in the history of North America. It was led by an enslaved blacksmith named Gabriel Prosser. He planned an uprising that would free the enslaved and kill the enslavers. In the name of freedom. But these plans were blown by two enslaved people who were more loyal to their enslavers than to the hope of liberation.

This failed revolt left enslavers scared that they would be next, and that they might not get tipped off first. So what did they do? You guessed it, the enslavers came up with even more racist ideas to protect White lives.

6

Words vs. Actions
1801–1826

WHEN THOMAS JEFFERSON BECAME PRESIDENT IN 1801, there was lots of talk and debate over what to do about the issue of slavery. One idea tossed around by White assimilationists was for Black people to "go back" to Africa and the Caribbean. But Black people didn't want to "go back" to a place that many had never known. Their ancestors had been captured from Africa and brought to North America, where generations of Black people were born. They'd built America as enslaved people and wanted what they were owed. Freedom in the country they'd built. America was now their land.

Do you see how racist ideas of today are tied to racist ideas of the past? The phrase "Go back to where you came from" that is sometimes said to Black and Brown people today connects to the "go back" idea of the past. Now you can trace the origins right back to Thomas Jefferson. (By the way, just imagine what Native Americans and Black people must have wished about their White oppressors: Can we send White people "back" to Europe?)

Let's
UNPAUSE

So President Jefferson's response to this debate was to put a policy in place that he thought might actually start the process of ending slavery. Remember, Jefferson's ideas about Black people were very confusing. When it came to the issue of slavery, President Jefferson's actions didn't match his words.

Jefferson's *words* seemed to be antislavery.

He wrote that "all men are created equal" in the Declaration of Independence. He said he wanted to send enslaved people "back" to Africa to be free. And he apologized for slavery and said it was wrong.

But Jefferson's *actions* seemed to be proslavery.

He enslaved hundreds of people because he felt he *needed* their labor to run his plantation. And only ever freed a few.

The contradictions are confusing, but one thing is clear: The issue of slavery was at the core of many of the decisions Jefferson made as president. In his life, he was a segregationist and an assimilationist, but he was never an antiracist.

As White people continued to seize land from Native Americans across the North American continent, decisions were made about whether slavery would be part of these new territories or states. And most of the time, the answer was yes. As the country grew bigger, discussions about ending slavery and sending enslaved people "back" grew smaller.

Because too much money was being made. And enslavers weren't willing to give that up to do what was right. Simple as that.

7

Words Matter

1831–1852

WORDS MATTER. THEY INFLUENCE WHAT WE THINK and how we act. So it comes as no surprise that ideas about Black people and slavery continued to be shared through writing. These writings almost always expressed ideas about Black people being *lesser* and White people being *greater*. But there are other examples that broke this trend.

For instance, William Lloyd Garrison. He was a White abolitionist who started a newspaper in 1831. He was inspired by Black abolitionists in Boston, people like Maria Stewart and David Walker. Like them, he believed in the immediate physical freedom of Black people. (Yes!) But his ideas involved Black people proving their equality to White people who, *eventually*, would accept their existence. (No!) To make it plain, he believed in, "Free today, but equal later on after White people are sure you deserve to be equal, because your being human isn't enough."

Black people shouldn't have to convince White people they are equal! His ideas about freedom for Black people had strings attached—requirements he felt Black people would have to meet. Because, apparently, being people wasn't enough. In 1835, Garrison shared his ideas about Black people and their freedom. He and others who joined him used the new technology of mass printing and the postal service to flood the nation with twenty to fifty thousand abolitionist pamphlets a week. A million antislavery pamphlets by the end of the year!

In 1845, there was a new narrative. Instead of this one giving thoughts and opinions about slavery, it was a firsthand account of its horrors. This story was written by Frederick Douglass, a Black man who had been enslaved. His book, *The Narrative of the Life of Frederick Douglass, an American Slave,* was published with Garrison's help. And it was a hit! An important weapon to fight against the idea that Black people were inferior. But Douglass was a runaway enslaved person whose voice was getting attention, which put him in danger of being caught. Although he had to flee to Great Britain and continue spreading his antislavery message there, his words and message became gold for all those who were working to abolish slavery in America.

Douglass's narrative wasn't the only story to describe what it was like to be enslaved. *The Narrative of Sojourner Truth* is another. Although women were also enslaved and enslavers, they were mostly left out of the discussion. Until this book. Sojourner Truth was bold. The kind of woman who would stand up in a room full of White people and declare her humanity. The kind of woman who used antiracist ideas to uplift *all* humanity.

White people were writing stories about slavery, too. One fictional narrative, titled *Uncle Tom's Cabin*, became one of the most popular books ever. Some of you may even have to read it in school at some point. The author, an abolitionist named Harriet Beecher Stowe, wrote the tale of an enslaved man who befriends a young White girl and holds tight to his Christian faith even as he is mistreated. The book was Stowe's attempt to use fiction to change White people's views about slavery. To try to help them understand its horrors. Still, there were a bunch of racist ideas in this story. So even while it inspired many readers to join the abolitionist movement, it also helped to strengthen ideas that Black people couldn't be as smart or as human as White people.

With antislavery books and ideas getting more popular, White people who were proslavery got busy spreading even more hate. They'd used literature and storytelling as a racist weapon by the invention of the "enslaver are do-gooders" narrative, and used math as a racist weapon in the past (remember that three-fifths of a person nonsense?), and now they would use science. Or fake science, anyway.

Yep, even scientists joined in on the racism and were now working to justify slavery. One scientist claimed that White people had bigger skulls than Black people and therefore more intelligence. A report claimed that free Black people had more mental health challenges than enslaved Black people, and that biracial people had shorter life spans than White people. Of course, none of this was true! But these racist lies were hidden behind "science" and used to support and spread fake ideas about Black people. Anything to justify supremacy and slavery. Anything to stop ideas about freedom.

Soon, there would be a new political leader to weigh in on the issue of slavery: Abraham Lincoln.

8

War over Slavery

1858–1867

WHAT COMES TO MIND WHEN YOU THINK ABOUT Abraham Lincoln?

> ✻ He was very tall.
> ✻ He wore a big black hat.
> ✻ We call him "honest Abe."
> ✻ He "freed the slaves."

Well, it's not quite that simple. Things never really are. People are complicated and flawed. Like, remember how Thomas Jefferson said "all men are created equal" but was also an enslaver who wrote racist ideas? Well, Abraham Lincoln said a lot of contradictory stuff, too. Like rope tied to a kite, he seemed to sway in different directions depending on where the wind blew.

Think about something you really wanted. A dog. A cell phone. A new video game. Maybe you made promises and did everything you could to persuade an adult to get it for you. Like, "I promise to walk the dog every day! Twice a day!" You made those promises even if you really didn't believe them yourself. You were only thinking, *What can I say to get the thing I want?* Lincoln was a lot like that. Except the kinds of promises he was making were about people's lives.

Before he ran for president, Lincoln tried to become a senator by being antislavery, but *not* antiracist. Here's what that meant.

Lincoln said he wanted slavery to end. Great!

Lincoln said he didn't think Black people should be treated as equal to White people. Not great.

Lincoln said slavery should end because if labor continued to be free, it would be bad for poor White people. Since they were too poor to own people, they would need to work. But how could they work if no one needed their labor because of enslavement? So it wasn't because slavery was horrible that Lincoln wanted it to end. He wanted to end it to help poor White people find work and make money.

None of this worked for enslavers. They, of course, did not want slavery to end. They wanted to remain wealthy. And because they had the power, Lincoln lost.

So to win the presidency, Lincoln made a different promise. A promise that would get racists to vote for him. That promise? He would stop all his talk about ending slavery. Lincoln won.

But even with this promise, enslavers didn't trust Lincoln. They didn't see him as Honest Abe at all! They worried that Lincoln was a threat to their wealth. They worried about more revolts by enslaved people. And so the southern states decided to break away from the nation and create their own separate territory. This territory, known as the Confederacy, would be led by its own president—someone who they believed would protect their wealth and their way of life. And to be clear: Their way of life was slavery.

America was now a country split in half. Two separate unions. Each with its own flag. Each operating with its own set of rules and laws. And each wanting the other to act a certain way. This was a *big* problem. And in 1861, a huge fight began over this division. This Civil War was not between America and another country. A war within our own country. Americans vs. Americans.

[Let's PAUSE]

Today there are people and history books that claim that the Civil War was not about slavery. And that symbols from this time, such as the Confederate flag and monuments of leaders of the Confederacy, are about southern pride. But the honest truth is the fighting, the war, the symbols, and the monuments *are* about White supremacy and racial terror. Today, many of those symbols and statues are being removed from public spaces. Because what they represent is that the southern states, the

Confederacy, did not want to give up slavery and the wealth and power it gave them. And they were willing to battle and shed blood to protect this.

[Let's
UNPAUSE]

To get the chance to fight against the thing that had been terrorizing them for centuries, enslaved people risked their lives and took any chance to run away to join the Union Army. At first, Union soldiers sent them right back, enforcing the Fugitive Slave Act, which said all runaway enslaved people had to be returned to their enslavers. But all that changed in the summer of 1862. The Union declared that those who escaped slavery to join the war would be "forever free." Then Lincoln made an even bigger declaration: that all enslaved people in Confederate areas would now be free. But you see the problem there? Lincoln's declaration did not free *all* enslaved people, only those in Confederate areas.

Enslaved people in other parts of the country would have to wait for the Thirteenth Amendment, which ended slavery throughout the United States.

For emancipated people who were now "free," freedom was complicated. Black people did not have the power to live fully, without limitations. To determine their own destiny. They were still caught in the tangled rope of racism.

TO BE FREE

Why was freedom complicated? Americans had a lot of different ideas about what freedom meant and who freedom was for.

The president of the Confederacy, a man named Jefferson Davis, said that inequality between Black and White people was "stamped from the beginning." Meaning that Black and White people never were and never could be considered equal. Four years after the Civil War started, the battle between the North and the South was over. The North had won and all enslaved people were declared "free," but freedom still felt far away. Because:

Black people were free...but they didn't have a place to go—they didn't have land of their own.

Black people were free...but they didn't have a way to earn money and build a life for themselves.

Black people were free...but they didn't have the tools White people had, such as access to schools or family money or privilege.

Black people were free...but they weren't allowed to vote.

Black people were free...but that didn't change how White people felt about them or treated them.

The South may have lost the war, but people were not willing to surrender their racist ideas.

q

To Be Free
1878–1903

IMAGINE ROPE BEING USED IN A GAME OF TUG-OF-WAR between two people. A brightly colored flag is tied to its center, and from opposite ends each person pulls until the flag and the majority of the rope are closest to their side.

Back then, W. E. B. Du Bois (rhymes with *voice*) and Booker T. Washington were two powerful Black leaders in a game of tug-of-war. Except it really wasn't a game. Both men were pulling for their ideas about freedom for Black people.

What were their ideas about? Education.

When Du Bois was ten (and still known as Willie), he was rejected by a girl on an interracial playground because she was White and he was Black. This racial experience was part of what drove him to compete with his White classmates. He wanted to convince them he was "not different." And if he *was* going to be different in any way, it would be because he was better.

Du Bois believed Black people should be educated. You may be thinking, of course everyone should be educated! But Du Bois didn't believe in education as a way for Black people to reach whatever goals they had in mind for themselves. He believed that if Black people got a college education, they would be more like White people. And if that happened, White people would accept them.

(What's that word again? The one to describe people who believe you can only be liked if you act like someone you're not? You got it: assimilationist.)

While he believed Black people should be educated, he also believed that only one in ten of them was cut out for learning. He thought only the exceptional "Talented Tenth" should get a college education and become leaders of the Black race, like him.

By now you're seeing that even leaders can be...well... downright confusing. Du Bois is another example. He was a Black man who, at times, didn't think much of... Black people.

On the other side of the tug-of-war rope was another powerful Black leader, Booker T. Washington. Washington believed that, for Black people, learning a trade like farming and carpentry was more important than going to college, and that Black people shouldn't try to become politicians or compete with White people. Washington felt Black people should just forget about political equality. Instead, they should be satisfied being thought of as less by White people, and become really good at trades such as farming and carpentry to win respect and acceptance.

Both Du Bois and Washington were assimilationists. Although they had this in common, they didn't like each other very much and argued over whose ideas were better. They both wrote popular books on their different ideas about education and freedom for Black people. Those ideas had something important in common: They said Black people couldn't just be themselves; they'd have to behave in ways that would be acceptable to White people.

10

Truth Tellers

1890-1911

ANOTHER THING BOTH DU BOIS AND WASHINGTON definitely agreed on was that Black people were not totally innocent when it came to White people punishing them harshly.

Yep. You read that right.

It took a young antiracist Black woman to set these men straight. A woman who believed that freedom had to include justice and equality. Her name was Ida B. Wells-Barnett.

Racist ideas have lived in people's minds for hundreds of years. But all along the way, there were people who had antiracist ideas. Pay close attention to them. They are like guideposts that have shown us the way from the beginning; they guide us even today.

Remember that thing about rope I mentioned at the beginning of this journey? How it can be used to tie, pull, hold, and lift? Well, sometimes, rope can also be used as a weapon. Used to create nooses to hang, or lynch, people. What's lynching? It was a way to permanently punish Black people by killing them as "punishment" for crimes they often did not commit. It was done to remind Black people that White people had complete power over them, even to end their lives. Wells-Barnett was a journalist who investigated lynchings. Like other leaders, Wells-Barnett used writing to share her ideas. Wells-Barnett exposed the truth. She stood up against racist terror when Black male leaders, including W. E. B. Du Bois, would not.

While others spent their lives tied to assimilationist and racist ideas, Ida B. Wells-Barnett was anchored by ideas that were antiracist. She said, "The way to right wrongs is to turn the light of truth upon them." She turned the light of truth on all racist wrongs.

Later, she would use those ideas in the suffrage movement, which helped women get the right to vote with the passing of the Nineteenth Amendment to the Constitution. But by "women," the country meant *White* women. And again, Wells-Barnett worked tirelessly to challenge this, to remind people that Black women must also be included.

Another person who tried to set Du Bois straight was Franz Boas, a German immigrant who had become one of America's most important anthropologists, an expert on what makes human beings human. He pointed out the history of Black people before they got to America. And how that history—African history—wasn't one of inferiority. Instead it was one of glorious empires, like those of Ghana, Mali, and Songhay, full of intellects and innovators.

These antiracist truth tellers battled with racist liars. Remember that freedom in the United States, liberation for all, has been a constant battle.

Between enslavers and those enslaved.

Between the Union (North) and the Confederacy (South).

Between leaders filled with contradictions and leaders free of them.

Between racism and antiracism.

There have been people pulling at one end of the rope for freedom and those pulling at the other end for oppression. And they used every tool imaginable. They used writing and books. They used weapons and war. They used speeches and activism. They used laws and education. And as technology evolved, they'd also use movies.

II

Racism On-Screen
1912–1915

THINK ABOUT THE POWER OF STORIES. OUR FAVORITE characters make us feel brave and better about ourselves and the world. Great stories change and challenge us. They make us want to be great, too. Another kind of power stories have is that they get inside our hearts and minds and stick around for a long, long time. Sometimes we may read stories without realizing the harm they cause, without recognizing racist ideas inside them. And because stories stick, those ideas can get tangled up inside us.

Like *Tarzan of the Apes.*

You may know the animated version shown today. It all began with a book in 1912. Here's the basic plot:

1. A White child named John is orphaned in central Africa.
2. John is raised by apes.
3. The apes change his name to Tarzan, which means "white skin."
4. Tarzan becomes the best hunter and warrior. Better than all the Africans.
5. Eventually he teaches himself to read.
6. In later stories in the series, Tarzan protects a White woman named Jane from the "savage" Africans.

Now, you know that slavery has ended at this point. But remember the ridiculous and racist idea that Africans *needed* slavery because they were "savages"? See how this popular book and later movies (and later comic strips, television shows, and even toys) support that idea?

Here's another way that stories are used to make racist ideas stick. In stories, animals can become symbols for an entire racial group. It's a way of saying the people of that group *are* animals. This is stereotyping. And one long-lasting racist stereotype is the comparison of Black people's facial features to those of monkeys and apes.

Remember the ridiculous and racist idea that Africans *needed* slavery because they were "savage animals" that needed taming? Not people but property, like horses and hogs? See how this all connects, even after slavery ended?

There was another movie that made racist ideas and stereotypes stick.

The Birth of a Nation.

Released in 1915, it was Hollywood's first blockbuster film (it was three hours long!) and was also the first-ever film that was screened at the White House for a president. Here's the basic plot:

1. A Black man (played by a White man in blackface) tries to attack a White woman.
2. She jumps off a cliff and dies.
3. Angry White men seek revenge for her death.

Oh, and those angry White men? They were called Klansmen.

The Ku Klux Klan (the KKK) is a racist terrorist organization that was formed by Confederate veterans after the Civil War. And they were reenergized by this movie, which glorified them and characterized Black people as dangerous and White people as saviors.

[Let's
PAUSE]

When the movie *The Birth of a Nation* was made, blackface had long been considered entertainment. White people darkened their faces with burnt cork or shoe polish. Then they performed in racist comedy acts, called minstrel shows, in theaters and in movies. They exaggerated Black facial features. Made big lips and noses. They created racial stereotypes by singing and dancing in ways that portrayed

Black people as lazy, unintelligent, sneaky cowards—all to amuse White audiences.

$$\begin{bmatrix} \text{Let's} \\ \text{UNPAUSE} \end{bmatrix}$$

Racial stereotypes in stories and movies have not only been about Black people. And this hasn't only occurred in the past, this continues to happen today.

Like in *King Kong. Dumbo. Peter Pan. Lady and the Tramp. The Cat in the Hat* and many books by Dr. Seuss. *Swiss Family Robinson. The Jungle Book. Little House on the Prairie. Curious George. Aladdin. Pocahontas.*

As truth seekers, you know how important it is to know the truth. And the truth is that many books and movies that are considered "classics" have racist ideas baked right into them. This matters because words matter. And stories are powerful. The images on the page and screen become the images in our minds, shaping the ways we see ourselves and think about people.

They reinforce what we come to believe is "normal" or "other."

So pay attention to words, stories, and movies. Look out for the ways they depict individuals and groups of people. Look out for the ways they can spread damaging ideas that mislead us about the world. And challenge those ideas with antiracist ones. Look out, also, for the many powerful stories that depict us all as we truly are—human.

12

Free to Be
1916–1936

As MOVIES CONTINUED TO PUSH RACIST IDEAS THAT put Black people's lives at risk, and the United States and its allies battled enemy nations in World War I, Black people from the South fled like refugees in their own country. They headed north. To Chicago. To Detroit. To New York. In search of freedom. They didn't know what opportunities were waiting for them there, but they had to take their chances. The chance to work. The chance to vote. The chance to live.

Some even came north from the Caribbean for the chance to escape colonialism. Like a Jamaican man named Marcus Garvey. The first thing Garvey did when he arrived, in 1916, was visit the NAACP office. The mission of the National Association for the Advancement of Colored People (NAACP) was stated in its name: to advance (or improve) the lives of Black people. And one of the founders of this organization was W. E. B. Du Bois.

At the NAACP office, Garvey noticed that no one dark-skinned worked there, and that Du Bois's vision also seemed to include colorism.

Let's
PAUSE

Word check! *Colorism* is discrimination against those with darker skin in favor of those with lighter skin. It is tied to racism because of the idea that the lighter the skin, the more intelligent and beautiful and better a person is. All because light skin is closer to White skin.

Remember how Du Bois and Washington were in a game of tug-of-war, which wasn't really a game, over their ideas about education and freedom for Black people? Now Du Bois and Garvey would quickly become the new players. But instead of battling over ideas for education, they battled over Blackness.

Du Bois was a light-skinned biracial Black man. Garvey was a dark-skinned Black man. Du Bois was an assimilationist. He believed that only some Black people had value. Garvey was an antiracist. He believed that all Black people were valuable.

So Garvey started his own organization, called the Universal Negro Improvement Association (UNIA). Its purpose was to focus on African solidarity, the beauty of dark skin and African American culture, and global African self-determination.

But remember, also, that people aren't just one way; they can be complicated and full of contradictions. In many ways, Du Bois made antiracist strides even while holding on to assimilationist ideas. For example, Du Bois noticed that the country thought of Black men as good enough to fight as soldiers—skilled, smart, brave—in World War I, but not good enough to be treated equally to White people back at home. He began to speak out against this contradiction. In a collection of essays, Du Bois wrote about the humanity of Black people. He also honored Black women. This was a huge deal, because Black women were unsung heroes who had been completely left out of the race conversation. But though he made antiracist strides, it was difficult for Du Bois to let go of his assimilationist ideas. He still believed that if Black people spoke, dressed, and behaved in ways that were acceptable to White people, then they would be accepted.

AN AWAKENING

The Harlem Renaissance was a time of renewal of Black creativity and culture. The music, paintings, and writings of young Black artists in Harlem, New York, would create a new African American identity. There were many contributors to this cultural explosion.

Writers such as Zora Neale Hurston and Langston Hughes.

Performers such as Josephine Baker and Paul Robeson.

Musicians such as Billie Holiday and Duke Ellington.

Artists such as Augusta Savage and Aaron Douglas.

As well as intellectuals such as Marcus Garvey and W. E. B. Du Bois.

Still tied to assimilationist ideas, Du Bois wanted these talented young Black artists to use their art to get White people to respect them—to be seen as perfect.

Black artists wanted the freedom to be imperfect—to be human.

Black people have always resisted racist ideas. Even when it was Black people who pushed them.

And there were Black people who rejected Du Bois's racist ideas. They believed they should be able express themselves however they wanted, as whole humans, without worrying about White acceptance. Like Langston Hughes. He was the most popular poet of the Harlem Renaissance and remains one of America's most celebrated poets. He declared that if Black artists leaned toward Whiteness, their art would not truly be their own. Hughes believed that Black people were beautiful. Just as they are.

But no matter how Black people spoke, dressed, wrote, painted, danced, or how much they educated themselves, White people continued to spread racist ideas and saw Black people as less human. Slowly worn down from this painful realization, Du Bois began to change. He began to want Black people to have the freedom to be Black. And for that to be enough.

Du Bois argued that the American educational system was failing the country because it wouldn't tell the truth about race in America. Because it was too concerned with protecting and defending the White race. He published an article called "Segregation," which shocked everyone. In it, he agreed with his former rival Marcus Garvey. Du Bois argued for the importance of Black safe spaces. Spaces where Black people could resist and fight against racist ideas. Ultimately, Du Bois was arguing for ideas he'd held in the past, but in new ways. In ways that Frederick Douglass, Sojourner Truth, Ida B. Wells-Barnett, Marcus Garvey, and many others before him had argued: that Black people were humans.

Du Bois had an awakening. He had turned away from assimilation and finally turned toward antiracism.

13

New Laws

1945–1960

AFTER THE HARLEM RENAISSANCE AND HIS OWN awakening, after the United States had entered into and emerged from World War II, Du Bois attended the Fifth Pan-African Congress. Pan-Africanism is a movement that encourages unity among all people of African descent. Strength in numbers. Global power. At this Fifth Pan-African Congress, members discussed the collective experiences of African descendants and the independence of African countries under European colonial control. Africans governing themselves.

Because of his work on behalf of Black people and African nations, Du Bois became known as the "father of Pan-Africanism."

During this time, America rose as a global leader. The words of the national anthem proudly proclaimed America's greatness:

The land of the free,

Home of the brave.

But who was brave enough to admit the truth about racism? A better question is, what did freedom really mean? Freedom for whom? So far, the answers had been freedom that was free for White people. And a fractured kind of freedom for Black people.

Lawyers were battling in court to address questions about freedom and equality. Some of those cases went to the Supreme Court, "the highest court in the land," where judges have the final say on American laws.

One case was about where Black people were allowed to buy homes. It exposed that in northern cities, White people were stopping Black people from living where they wanted to live. White people kept

Black people from buying houses in "their" neighborhoods. The Supreme Court ruled that creating segregated neighborhoods was against the law. Which made White people mad.

So mad that as Black people moved into "their" neighborhoods, they packed up and left, finding new ways to keep neighborhoods segregated.

Let's [PAUSE]

Back then, the Supreme Court ruled that housing segregation and segregated schools were against the law. And yet, today, segregated neighborhoods and schools still exist all over the country. There are still all-White (or almost all-White) neighborhoods and schools. There are still all-Black (or almost all-Black) or non-White neighborhoods and schools.

Remember that racism was stamped into America's design. And even though there have

$$\left[\begin{array}{c} \text{Let's} \\ \text{UNPAUSE} \end{array} \right]$$

Another case was about segregated schools in the South. Black students attended schools that were under resourced. There wasn't enough money to build or maintain schools, school buses, and for materials such as books, desks, and chairs. White students went to schools that were well resourced. Their schools were spacious and well maintained, and there was enough money for school buses and supplies. The Supreme Court ruled that segregation in public schools was unconstitutional, against the law. But a racist idea was part of this ruling. It was decided that Black students would integrate into White schools. But White students did not have to integrate into Black schools. This reinforced the racist idea that White people are superior—that for Black kids to succeed, *they* needed to be around White kids. Either way, this also made White people mad.

So mad that when Black students showed up at "their" schools, mobs of White people showed up, too.

So mad they screamed, called Black students horrible names, spat on them, and threatened their lives, whether they were high school students or first-graders like Ruby Bridges.

So mad that six-year-old Ruby had to be escorted to school each day by federal marshals who protected her from the mobs of angry White people she had to pass to enter the building.

So mad that White parents refused to let their children be in the same class with Ruby. Or eat lunch with her. Or play with her at recess. Ruby was taught in a classroom alone while federal marshals guarded the door.

See, laws alone are not powerful enough to create freedom for all. For freedom to exist for everyone, it takes people to fight for the *right* laws that benefit *all* people, and make sure those laws are followed.

14

Fighting for Freedom

1955–1963

THE CIVIL RIGHTS MOVEMENT WAS SPARKED BY THE deaths of Black people at the hands of White people who refused to follow the law, and who decided what freedom meant and who freedom was for. And for whom it wasn't.

Like fourteen-year-old Emmett Till.

In 1955, Emmett was brutally beaten and killed for supposedly "hissing" or "whistling" at a White woman. What happened to Emmett Till over sixty-five years ago is something that still hurts the hearts of Black people today. He was a boy who had his whole life ahead of him when it was so viciously taken away. For Black people, Emmett was their son. Brother. Neighbor. The pain of his loss feels that close. For Black people, Emmett's death was a reminder that in America, the land of the free, Black people could only live a lesser version of freedom.

Back then, Emmett's murder lit a fire under the civil rights movement that was led by a young, charismatic preacher who admired Du Bois. Someone I bet you've heard of. Dr. Martin Luther King Jr.

Along with Dr. King, there were many young people who had new ways of fighting for freedom that helped the civil rights move-ment grow more

and more powerful. Like the four college students who sat down at a "Whites only" lunch counter in North Carolina in 1960. They were denied service, but they stayed there until the store closed. This kind of protest was called a "sit-in," and within a few months, students all across the South were doing it.

Young people organized and established the Student Nonviolent Coordinating Committee (SNCC) to plan peaceful protests.

But the response to the *nonviolent* civil rights movement was...*violence.*

In southern states like Alabama, racist laws and those sworn to protect them were weapons that harmed Black lives. Dr. King organized nonviolent protests in the city of Birmingham, Alabama. The commissioner of public safety used his power to order the police to beat and set attack dogs loose on protesters. He ordered the fire departments to turn water hoses on them. And he had protesters arrested, including Dr. King. He used his powers to make sure Birmingham would remain segregated.

It would take Dr. King, SNCC, and the power of a whole lot of people to keep the civil rights movement going. To fight for freedom for Black people. To fight for freedom for all.

15

March on Washington
1963

THE NATION AND THE WORLD WATCHED NONVIOLENT protests become violent—not by the actions of protesters, but by police. Many battle-worn young activists became frustrated. They were frustrated by Dr. Martin Luther King Jr.'s faith in nonviolence, because Black people were being beaten, jailed, and killed. Many started listening to another leader: Malcolm X.

Malcolm X was a minister in the Nation of Islam, a religious organization focused on the liberation of Black people.

Martin and Malcolm, like Du Bois and Washington and later Du Bois and Garvey, were two Black leaders in another game of tug-of-war. Martin and Malcolm both wanted freedom and equality for Black people. But each leader had different ideas about how Black people should fight for their freedom.

Martin preached nonviolence as a tool for overcoming oppression.

Malcolm preached self-defense and freedom by any means necessary.

Dr. King and other activists had been working with political leaders to pass civil rights laws. They planned a huge televised rally for August 28, 1963, in Washington, DC—the March on Washington for Jobs and Freedom. This would be an opportunity for Dr. King to convince the nation of the importance and urgency of civil rights.

During this time, John F. Kennedy was president. Although the event was organized by civil rights groups, President Kennedy's administration knew the world would be watching. So they approved the speakers and the speeches. Which meant there were some who got a microphone—whose voices were heard—but many others who were silenced by the White House and by Black male leaders of the civil rights movement.

Like...

Black women. Daisy Bates read a short vow, a pledge on behalf of women working within the movement. But Dorothy Height, a powerful leader who helped organize the event and was the only woman to stand on the platform with Dr. King, was not invited to speak. Nor was Rosa Parks. Or so many other Black women whose work had fueled the movement.

Black LGBTQ+ leaders. Bayard Rustin, a key adviser to Dr. King and an organizer of the event, was not invited to speak. Nor was James Baldwin, a Black novelist who, through his writings, had become a brilliant and bold political voice.

Malcolm X. He attended the event but was not invited to speak.

But a Black woman did sing. Mahalia Jackson. As the civil rights movement pushed on, Jackson had been using her voice to lift the spirits of Black people across the segregated South. In fact, Dr. King himself would call Jackson whenever he felt discouraged, just to hear her sing. And on this day, she sang and encouraged the nation.

At the March, approximately 250,000 activists and reporters from around the world walked to the area between the Lincoln Memorial and the Washington Monument. And on this day, Dr. King gave what is known today as one of the greatest speeches of all time: "I Have a Dream."

16

Pain and Protest
1963–1965

A FEW WEEKS AFTER THE MARCH ON WASHINGTON for Jobs and Freedom, tragedy struck again. Four girls were killed in Birmingham, Alabama: Cynthia Wesley. Carole Robertson. Carol Denise McNair. Addie Mae Collins. White supremacists and members of the KKK bombed their church.

Again, the nation and the world watched. Outrage spread.

Angela Davis, who grew up in Birmingham, was a college student studying in Europe when she heard the news. Her family had been close friends with the Robertson family. She lived in the same neighborhood as the Wesley family. Davis did not see this moment as a one-off incident. The KKK bombed her neighborhood so often that it was nicknamed Dynamite Hill. She had grown up fully aware of American racism and its deadly potential. All she could do was use the news of this tragedy as fuel to keep fighting.

Alabama Church Blast--
4 Black Girls Blown Up

Birmingham Dynamiting
Triggers Violence---
2 Boys Shot to Death

The outrage over the murder of four little girls at a church was so great that the government was forced to take action. The Civil Rights Act of 1964 was passed into legislation. But what did it really mean? On paper, it made it a law that discrimination on the basis of race was illegal. Malcolm X spoke out not against the bill but about the likelihood of the law actually ever being enforced. Angela Davis felt the same way.

Because laws alone have never been powerful enough to create freedom for all. Who was going to make sure the laws would be followed if the law, lawmakers, and law enforcers were all racist?

Today, activist Angela Davis reminds us, "Freedom is a constant struggle." That it takes more than laws to bring about freedom for all. It takes people power to imagine and build a movement for all humanity.

Police brutality continued. The KKK continued. Job, housing, and education discrimination continued. Black political movements were not satisfied with what the government was doing for Black people. So protests continued. But without power, all the protesting in the world meant nothing. So there was a shift from fighting for civil rights to fighting for freedom. The difference between the two is simple. One is a fight for fairness. The other, a right to live.

And as they fought for the right to live, death would strike again.

This time, Malcolm X was assassinated.

His death rocked his Black antiracist followers. The media portrayed him as a messenger of hate. But

Malcolm's autobiography, published after his death, showed that Malcolm X was for truth, not hate. His message to Black people was about pride and unity. His autobiography would become one of the most important books in American history.

Dr. King and Malcolm X met only once. But Dr. King acknowledged that, though they had different methods—much like Du Bois and Washington, and Du Bois and Garvey—they really wanted the same thing: freedom.

After the Civil Rights Act, which Malcolm distrusted, came the Voting Rights Act of 1965. And what did it cause? White rage and resistance. However, the Voting Rights Act would become the most effective piece of antiracist legislation ever passed by the Congress of the United States of America.

Malcolm X was gone but not forgotten. His words continued to feel like an armor of protection from anti-Blackness, for young Black activists. And, for many, they still do.

17

Black Power
1966-1969

MATH. SCIENCE. ART. EACH HAS BEEN USED AS A weapon against Black people. But words, when spat from a racist tongue, have often been the most deadly.

You've heard that saying: "Sticks and stones can break my bones, but words will never hurt me." It means physical violence is more harmful than attacks on our feelings. But words *do* matter. They *do* hurt. Everyday words and phrases such as *black sheep, blackmail, blacklist,* and others connect Blackness with badness. They support the idea that black is negative. And other words help to suggest this. Such as *minority,* which suggests that Black people are minor, making White people major. And *ghetto*, a term used to describe an undesirable area of a city. In racist America, *ghetto* and *minority* became synonyms for *Black*. These words were used like knives, to inflict pain and suggest danger. They are still used this way today.

But at a rally in 1966, words were used as armor to fight *against* racism. Stokely Carmichael, the bold, new young leader of the Student Nonviolent Coordinating Committee (SNCC), shouted...

BLACK POWER!

These words connected Blackness not to negativity but to strength. "Black Power" was new language that

empowered the Black community and sparked a new movement.

Here's what Carmichael meant by Black Power:

Black people owning and controlling their own neighborhoods and futures, free of White supremacy.

Here's what racist White people and media heard:

BLACK SUPREMACY!

See what was happening? People afraid of antiracist ideas purposely twisted Carmichael's message of empowerment into racist ideas. And once again, there were Black leaders on opposite sides of the tug-of-war rope, pulling for different ideas about freedom. Assimilationists versus antiracists.

But a revolution had been sparked within the Black community. Which brings us to the Black Panther Party. Not like Marvel's Black Panther (Wakanda Forever!), but a movement sparked by Black Power. Huey Newton and Bobby Seale, leaders of the Black Panther Party, developed a list of goals to explain what they were fighting for on behalf of Black people. Their goals included:

FAIR HOUSING

ANTIRACIST
EDUCATION

AN END
TO POLICE
BRUTALITY

PEACE

Their overall goal was to fuel Black people's survival, success, and freedom.

One way they set about achieving this was through their free breakfast program for children. Fed up by the nation's neglect of Black people, the Black Panther Party fed tens of thousands of hungry children themselves. With donations received from local businesses and grocery stores, they served breakfast to children in churches and community centers before their school days began and even during the summers. *Self-reliance* was a word that mattered to the Black Panther Party—relying on the resources and power within the community. The popularity of the Black Panther Party's free breakfast program put pressure on the government. This led to the government's School Breakfast Program, which, even today, provides millions of children with breakfast at school.

18

History Repeats

1968

THE BLACK PANTHER PARTY AND THE BLACK POWER movement ramped up and spread out. Angela Davis joined the movement.

Even Dr. King, who at times expressed assimilationist thoughts, was drawn to it. He began to focus on getting the government to pass laws that would provide jobs and better housing for poor Black people set back by centuries of racism—ideas that were similar to some of the goals of the Black Panther Party.

White rage and fear also ramped up. And the old strategy of using stories to spread racist messages continued. This time with a new movie called *Planet of the Apes*.

Here's the basic plot:

1. White astronauts land on a planet after a two-thousand-year journey.
2. Apes enslave them.
3. Turns out, they're not on a faraway planet at all. They're on Earth.

[**Let's PAUSE**]

Remember that stories (even fictional ones) stick, and racist ideas can get tangled up inside of us? And how animals can be used to represent race, to stereotype? Like comparing Black people to monkeys and apes?

Are you putting this all together?

[**Let's UNPAUSE**]

Tarzan put the racist idea of White people needing to conquer Africa and Africans on the big screen. *Planet of the Apes* put the racist fear of the "dark" world rising against the White conqueror on the big screen. *Planet of the Apes* was a blockbuster. Like *Tarzan* and *The Birth of a Nation*, it became part of popular culture. It encouraged White people to be afraid and to arm themselves, and was a warning to Black people to "stay in their place."

The American government helped to spread this message, expressing the need to "protect" citizens (White citizens) against the Black Panther Party. The words the government used to label the Black Panther Party were *militant, radical, dangerous*.

The rallying cry "Black Power" was portrayed as a racist phrase.

Then tragedy struck again. (AGAIN!)

Reverend Dr. Martin Luther King Jr. was assassinated.

Again the collective hearts and spirits of Black people were broken. But it wasn't just the nation that grieved. Dr. King was the leader of one of the largest movements for equality and humanity that the world had ever seen. He'd won the Nobel Peace Prize for his courageous non-violent leadership. He was a global inspiration.

The whole world wept.

Dr. King's death inspired a rally like none other, and Black Power grew into the largest American antiracist movement ever.

SAY IT LOUD!
I'M BLACK AND I'M PROUD!

In 1968, the song "Say it Loud—I'm Black and I'm Proud" by James Brown became an anthem that inspired Black people to reclaim Black pride. Dark skin and Black hair were proudly embraced as beautiful. African clothing was popular. There was a demand for Black studies at colleges and in K-12 schools. Antiracists of all racial and ethnic backgrounds joined the movement.

The Black Power movement was powerful but not perfect. Men ran it. Women were pushed to the back.

But Black women have always risen. Black women like...

- ✸ **Fannie Lou Hamer**, a community and women's rights activist who fought fiercely for civil rights, voting rights, and greater economic opportunities for Black people.
- ✸ **Diane Nash**, a founding member of SNCC, who led sit-ins at lunch counters and organized Freedom Rides across the South.
- ✸ **Angela Davis**, an activist, educator, and influential advocate for political and social change.

Even when pushed to the back, Black women have led the resistance. As the movement continued to grow, women found new ways and new groups to lead.

19

Antiracism Rising
1968-1982

THE FIGHT FOR CIVIL RIGHTS CONTINUED IN THE UNITED States, capturing the attention of the world. Politicians continued to use segregationist ideas to win votes. So when presidential candidate Richard Nixon started his campaign in 1968, he figured he could win by getting segregationists and racists on his side. But now it wasn't easy to be so obvious about racist ideas. Remember, the world was watching. So how did he do it? Well, he used words.

Nixon used coded words that represented racist ideas. Words and phrases like *ghetto*, *undesirables*, and *dangerous elements*. Without ever actually saying Black people, he was able to communicate racist ideas to White people, who understood exactly what (and who) he was talking about. And he used words to misrepresent the protests happening around the nation. He portrayed them as dangerous in order to shut them down. His plan was called the "southern strategy." And it worked.

Nixon won.

Meanwhile, Angela Davis continued to use words to inspire antiracism and take action against injustices. She began speaking out about Black people who she believed were wrongly put in prison. Some were Black Power activists. Her actions caught the attention of the government, which did everything it could to stop her. Including putting her in jail for a crime she did not commit. But Davis studied the law, and she studied her case. After a year and a half in prison, her trial began. She represented herself.

Davis won!

Angela Davis was free from jail. But she was not free. Not truly free. She was an antiracist who understood that freedom means freedom for all, not for one. So she

continued to fight for freedom for all Black people. And she wasn't alone.

Audre Lorde. Ntozake Shange. Alice Walker. Michele Wallace. Black feminists wrote poems, stories, and books that captured their existence and made sure they were seen, heard, and not forgotten. Their work challenged the attempts of anyone who tried to silence Black women and the LGBTQ+ community.

In addition to the writings of Black feminists, there was another important story. So important that it became a miniseries that was shown on television. Alex Haley's *Roots: The Saga of an American Family* told the story of what enslavement was really like. It disrupted the racist ideas that Black people were enslaved because they were less human and White people who were enslavers were kind. Slavery was cruel and inhumane. Period.

Through words, stories, and books, antiracist ideas were spreading.

But racist ideas kept spreading, too.

20

Fight the Power
1971-1994

MORE POLITICIANS FOUND THEY COULD BECOME successful using race to win votes and by pushing racist laws and policies. Laws are the rules you get punished for breaking, and policies are the practices and procedures that shape how things are done. The kind of laws and policies these politicians were making created BIG problems for Black people.

Like...

✻ The War on Drugs pushed by President

Ronald Reagan. Even though White people and Black people were selling and using drugs at similar rates, the new drug laws targeted Black people. For example, one law made it a more serious crime to be caught with small amounts of the types of drugs more often found in poor Black neighborhoods than with larger amounts of the types of drugs more often found in rich White neighborhoods. The result of this new policy was that millions of Black Americans were sent to jail. It was a war on Black people, and it devastated Black communities.

- Presidential candidate George H. W. Bush, who used the racist idea that Black people are a threat, to help win the presidency.
- The Violent Crime Control and Law Enforcement Act by the administration of President Bill Clinton that caused the largest increase of the prison population in United States history. Mostly for nonviolent crimes. Mostly Black men. Which reinforced the

racist ideas that "Black people are violent" and "Black people are mostly criminals."

[Let's PAUSE]

You're probably wondering a few things. Like, why would anyone, especially the president of the United States, do these things? Remember, racist ideas have been stamped into the way the country runs since the beginning. And racist ideas have often been stamped into the hearts and minds of people who run it. Also, racist ideas have created privileges and wealth for White people.

And you're also probably wondering, how do we stop this? We do so by doing what you're doing right now. We do it by learning the history of racist ideas. By recognizing the pattern of racist ideas of the past and connecting them to what you see happening in the present. By reading, thinking, and questioning. And by

challenging racist ideas with antiracist ones.
Dismantling racist laws and policies. By daring
to imagine a new and antiracist future.

$$\Big[\substack{\text{Let's} \\ \textbf{UNPAUSE}} \Big]$$

But Black people, as always, pressed on. Pushed
against the hate. And during this time, they would beat
racism back with...a beat.

Hip-hop became the drumbeat for change and
empowerment. Songs like Public Enemy's "Don't Believe
the Hype" and "Fight the
Power" were a force. For
young Black people, those
words weren't just titles, they
were anthems. They gave a

feeling of Black power and pride. They called for Black people to resist racism and oppression. These songs were a protest of their own, a powerful critique of mainstream America and a reminder that the revolution for freedom had not ended.

Rappers like Queen Latifah uplifted young Black women with her blockbuster album *All Hail the Queen*. Her song "Ladies First" was about women's empowerment. It spoke back to oppressors who tried to make women small. Women like Queen Latifah, MC Lyte, and Salt-N-Pepa all commanded space on the hip-hop stage.

Hip-hop spoke to a new generation of Black youth that was frustrated about racist mistreatment. Like what happened to Rodney King, a twenty-five-year-old Black man who was beaten by Los Angeles police officers. It was not the first time a Black person was attacked by the police, but it was one of the first times the beating was captured on video (this was before smartphones) and shared widely. The officers were charged but found not guilty.

Black Americans were angry. And in pain. So pained and angered that they took over neighborhoods in Los

Angeles and expressed their frustrations. Dr. King once said, "A riot is the language of the unheard." Frustrated, angry, and unheard, Black people burned stores and took merchandise. About ten thousand National Guard troops were brought in to stop the uprisings.

Even as Black people continued to resist, *more* (there's always MORE!) racist laws and policies were created to convince a new generation of Americans of the idea that Black people, not racism, were the problem.

21

Unequal Tests

2002

YEARS AFTER DESEGREGATION BECAME THE LAW OF the land (on paper if not in practice), racists found a new way to make public education a weapon: standardized testing. You probably know a lot about standardized tests. The kind kids take each year, especially in public schools, where they must write short essays and fill in the bubbles for answer A, B, C, or D to questions about reading comprehension, writing, math, and science.

They are "standardized," meaning that the same test is given to all kids in a state, no matter where they live or go to school. And, of course, this is exactly why they aren't fair.

Here's the thing: *Equality* and *equity* are two words that look similar, but there is an important difference between them, especially when it comes to education. Equality is about kids having the same access. *Equity* is about kids having access *and* what *they* need to learn.

Standardized tests, while given equally, are not equitable.

Because they were never created with each student in mind.

Because they treat all students as if they are the same and have the same resources.

But the test results in underfunded and segregated schools (which of course aren't as good as results in schools where students have lots of resources!) are used to support the age-old racist idea that Black people aren't as smart as White people; that Black and White people are biologically different. And politicians found ways to place even more importance on these unfair tests, setting it up so that schools that got better results were rewarded with more resources.

Which is a way of making sure the rich get richer and the poor get poorer.

And while mostly Black and Brown students were hurting from this policy, segregationists and assimilationists argued that the way to fix racism was to simply stop focusing on it.

$$\left[\begin{array}{c}\textbf{Let's}\\\textbf{PAUSE}\end{array}\right]$$

The idea that we should pretend NOT to see racism is connected to the idea that we should pretend NOT to see color. It's called color-blindness. Not the medical condition whereby it's hard for some people to tell the difference between red and green. But the kind where people think it's better to act like they don't see differences in skin color. Here's what's WRONG with this.

✳ It's ridiculous! Skin color is something we all absolutely see.

✳ It's dark skin that people pretend not

to see, which reinforces the idea that something is wrong with Black skin.

✴ If people do not see color, that means they do not see racism.

So to pretend not to see color is pretty convenient if you don't actually want to stamp out racism in the first place.

[Let's
UNPAUSE]

The No Child Left Behind Act put in place by President George W. Bush (son of President George H. W. Bush) actually left lots of kids behind. Black kids. This policy decreased funding to schools when students were not making improvements on standardized tests. Schools attended by mostly Black students were already underfunded and lacked the resources of schools attended by mostly White students. Once again, policies like this reinforced the racist idea that Black people—Black children—were the problem. Not racist policies.

22

A Black President
2005–2008

ANTIRACIST MOMENTUM WOULD NOT BE STOPPED. AT an important global conference, American activists like Angela Davis attended and made connections with activists from around the world. They wanted the conference to be the start of a global antiracist movement. Participants left the conference carrying the antiracist momentum with them. Back to Senegal. The United States. Japan. Brazil. France. Around the whole world.

Then a new Black political leader burst onto the scene. And guess what? He was seen as an exception. Remember how racists just couldn't believe the intelligence and talent of Phillis Wheatley, the poet? How they turned their backs on her and refused to publish her work? And remember how, at first, Du Bois believed only some African Americans, the Talented Tenth, were cut out for learning and leadership? Well, in 2005, almost 250 years after racists tried to dismiss Phillis Wheatley, Barack Obama was seen as the new "extraordinary" Black person. He became the country's fifth African American senator ever, and the only one serving at that time. And his success was used as a symbol of a "postracial" America—to claim that the country's long history of racism had ended. That racism no longer existed.

Using individual Black people as symbols has been a tool to suggest that they're "extraordinary" and "exceptional." It's a way of saying that they're "different" from and "better" than ordinary Black people. It's a way of saying that they have "overcome" being Black. Ultimately, it's a way of saying that being Black, and not racism, is the problem. White people refused to believe that all Black people could be as intelligent as Phillis Wheatley; they decided that she must be "extraordinary."

Here's another way that Black people are used as symbols. White people who deny that racism still exists point to the success of a small handful of Black people, such as Oprah Winfrey, Michael Jordan, and Barack Obama, as proof. It's like treating a few successful Black individuals as characters in a fictional story, and the setting is a country where race doesn't matter.

To tell an accurate story about the progress of Black people in the United States means looking at the whole group, not just a few individuals. And it means looking at all the systems in the nation—such as education, housing, and employment—to see if they're truly working for everyone, not just for some. It means not looking for an easy way to deny that racism is still very real. It means, instead, doing the work of antiracists to ensure freedom and equality exist for all.

But a natural disaster would make it very clear that racism did, in fact, still exist. Hurricane Katrina struck in the summer of 2005. It flooded the Gulf Coast, took the lives of more than 1,800 people, forced millions to migrate, and caused billions of dollars in property damage. Even in "color-blind" America, where White people claimed it was better NOT to see race, it was hard NOT to see how racism continued to destruct and destroy. You might be wondering, what does a hurricane have to do with racism? No one can control Mother Nature, right? Well…right. But what *can* be controlled is the response. Policies and practices *are* in people's control.

For years, scientists and journalists had warned that southern Louisiana, a region that was home to a large population of Black people, would be in danger if hit by a major hurricane. And no one did anything. Then, when Hurricane Katrina did hit, the Bush administration's response to this natural disaster was delayed, with devastating effects on the lives of the poor Black community living there.

Two years later, Barack Obama announced his candidacy for president. Racists tried to tear down Barack and his wife, Michelle. They were called unpatriotic for speaking honestly about racism in America or being associated with those who did. Opponents used coded language and racist imagery to belittle the Obamas and their accomplishments. Even Obama's nationality was challenged, a movement fueled by Donald Trump (who would later also become president). Trump, a businessman at the time, used his influence and resources to spread the racist idea that someone with a name like Barack Obama could not be a citizen of the United States. Because of these racist claims, Obama was pressured to share his birth certificate to prove his citizenship, unlike any White candidate.

On November 4, 2008, Angela Davis, recently retired as a professor, cast her vote for Barack Obama, as did roughly 69.5 million Americans. And he won. The first Black president of the United States!

When Obama was elected the forty-fourth president of the United States, happiness burst from all over the United States and spread around the antiracist world. People danced in the streets. Grassroots organizers had

succeeded. They showed people who didn't think a Black president could be elected that they were wrong. People rejoiced in the pride and victory for Black people. And people celebrated the antiracist potential of the nation's first Black president.

23

An Antiracist Movement

2009–2015

FOR MANY PEOPLE, PRESIDENT OBAMA WAS A SYMBOL of hope and progress. But by now you know that people aren't always just one way (like I've been saying this whole time). People can be complicated and contradictory (been saying that, too). Barack Obama, like leaders before him, such as Frederick Douglass, Abraham Lincoln, W. E. B. Du Bois, and Booker T. Washington, had moments when he expressed antiracist thoughts. But, under pressure, he also fell back on assimilationist ideas. And just as with Black leaders before him, assimilation didn't work.

Segregationists worked tirelessly to destroy and discredit him. They hurled insults about him and Black people. Racist politicians and media personalities spread racist ideas and stereotypes. Anything to crush the ego they assumed he had, being a Black president. Anything to try to "put him in his place."

And Black people continued to die. (See a pattern?)

Aiyana Jones. Trayvon Martin. Tamir Rice. Michael Brown. Black children's lives ended at the hands of police officers and those who placed no value on Black humanity. Black people's lives ended at the hands of police officers and White people who were rarely punished.

And just as in other parts of America's racist history, antiracists pushed from the margins to fight back once more. Or twice more. Or three, four, five, six, seven times more.

Black women like Alicia Garza, Patrisse Cullors, and Opal Tometi. They started not only a hashtag, #BlackLivesMatter, they started a movement.

#BlackLivesMatter was a direct response to police brutality. It was a rallying cry, a declaration of love, from the minds and hearts of three Black women—two

of whom are queer. It was an announcement to all that in order to be *truly* antiracist, we must also oppose *all* injustices, such as sexism, homophobia, colorism, and classism, that work alongside racism to harm so many Black lives.

In 2014, Black Lives Matter leaped from social media to protest signs and out of shouting mouths at antiracist uprisings across the country. These protesters rejected the racist declaration of six centuries: that Black lives don't matter. #BlackLivesMatter quickly transformed from an antiracist love declaration into an antiracist movement. A movement filled with young people operating in local BLM groups across the nation, often led by young Black women. Collectively, these activists were pulling against discrimination in all forms, in all areas of society.

And in response to those who acted as if Black male lives mattered the most, antiracist feminists boldly demanded of America to #SayHerName, to shine light on the women who have also been affected by the tangled mess of racism. Like antiracist daughters of Angela Davis, the activists of this new generation are symbols of hope, taking potential and turning it into power.

24

Black Lives Matter
2016–2020

IN 2016, THE PRESIDENTIAL ELECTION BETWEEN CANDIDATE Hillary Clinton and candidate Donald Trump shocked millions of people. Unlike presidential elections of the past, in which candidates felt they couldn't be so obvious about their racist ideas, that they instead needed to use coded language, Trump did the opposite. The nation listened as he spread racist ideas about Mexicans and Muslims. He promoted racist ideas all over the place, all while saying he wasn't racist when he was confronted.

It worked.

He won.

Trump quickly ushered in racist policies and practices. Immigration, for example. People living in the United States for years were sent back to the countries they were born in, forced to abruptly leave family and children behind. The Obama administration and presidents before him had also deported families crossing borders, sending them back to the countries they tried to escape for the chance of a better life in America. But under Trump's administration, countless families were torn apart at the border between Mexico and the United States. Children were separated from their parents and put into metal cages, waiting for a decision about what would happen next. At airports, Muslim citizens were blocked and sometimes banned from entering the country. Meanwhile, White immigrants from predominantly White countries didn't face the same discrimination and punishment.

These policies encouraged many Trump supporters and sparked hateful acts. Like in Charlottesville, Virginia. In 2017, hundreds of White supremacists who were angry about the removal of a Confederate statue gathered for a rally. Violence erupted. One person was killed, and many others were injured. Trump refused to say he disapproved of the rally and the actions of White supremacists.

Then, 2020. A global pandemic struck. The COVID-19 virus caused the deaths of hundreds of thousands of Americans. Again, race was at the core of this disaster. Trump's delayed response to COVID-19 resulted in Black, Latinx, and Indigenous people getting sick and dying at higher rates than White people. Lack of or limited access to health care prevented many people from receiving the help they needed. Many were deemed "essential workers" who had to risk exposure to the virus in order to keep their jobs, while people with higher-paying jobs safely sheltered in place at home. Businesses and the economy suffered. Many people lost their jobs. Going to school changed from being face-to-face in the classroom with teachers and peers to learning virtually at home.

But this wasn't the only plague spreading through the nation killing Black people.

———— •• ————

Ahmaud Arbery was chased and shot by White men while he was jogging. Breonna Taylor was shot by policemen in her own apartment. Then George Floyd. Killed on camera by a White police officer, sparking outrage that was fueled by frustration over the many Black people who were killed before him.

Again, antiracists fought back.

The Black Lives Matter movement responded and rallied, demanding justice for the Black men and women whose lives were ended by police brutality. This time, protests and uprisings spread across not only the nation but the world. People—organizing, protesting, working, and fighting. In the name of freedom. Protests led to widespread pledges by individuals and institutions for change.

The Black Lives Matter movement today is linked to the Black Power and civil rights movements of the past.

People. Fighting for laws that benefit all people.

People. Fighting to make sure those laws are followed.

People. Organizing, protesting, working, and fighting. In the name of freedom.

Because laws alone have never been powerful enough to create freedom for all—it's people who can bring about lasting change.

———◆◆◆———

In the midst of the 2020 global pandemic, there was another presidential election in the United States. Joe Biden, who had served as vice president under President Obama, was now running for president. And his running mate was a woman. A Black and Indian American woman whose parents were both immigrants, Kamala Harris.

Americans would again cast their vote for president of the United States. Black voters mobilized, and millions of Americans voted with freedom and justice in mind.

Biden and Harris won! Due in large part to the efforts and actions of Black people, and especially Black women, there would once again be a historic win for the United States. The first Black woman and South Asian American vice president, part of a team that beat Donald Trump, who promoted racism and White supremacy over and over. This victory might be a step in a more antiracist direction, but there's still a long road ahead.

Remember, this is more than just a past book. This is a present book, about the here and now. A book about every day. A book to help us learn about the history of racism in the United States. A book to help us think about ourselves and to understand that freedom and justice have to be fought for continuously. And it's up to us to continue this work. You may have learned some things in this book that make you look at your life differently. You may have learned about people and things you want to know a whole lot more about. So this book is a start, not a finish—keep reading, keep learning, and

KEEP TALKING ABOUT RACE.

From the beginning, racist ideas have been stamped into the United States—into the Constitution, laws, policies, practices, and beliefs of segregationists and assimilationists. Antiracists continue their work in helping us become tied to antiracist ideas and to use them to lift people up. Turning potential into power. People like Angela Davis. Like Patrisse Cullors. And, perhaps, like me and you.

AN ANTIRACIST FUTURE

Dear Reader,

How do you feel? I mean, I hope after reading this *present* book, you're left with some answers. I hope it's clear how the construct of race has always been used to gain and keep power. How it has always been used to create conditions that separate us to keep us quiet. To keep the ball of White and rich privilege rolling. And that it's not woven into people as much as it's woven into policy that people follow and believe is truth.

Laws that have kept Black people from freedom, from voting, from education, from housing, from health care, from shopping, from walking, from driving, from... breathing.

Laws that treat Black human beings like animals.

This is how racism works. And all it takes is the right kind of media—stories, movies, news shows—to spark it. To spin it. To make a great, big, tangled mess. This is what history has shown us. Tell a certain story a certain way. Make a movie that paints you as the hero. Get enough people on your side to tell you you're right, and you're right. Even if you're wrong. And once you've been told you're right long enough, and once your being right has led you to a profitable and privileged life, you'd do anything not to be proved wrong. Even pretend human beings aren't human beings.

From Zurara to Harriet Beecher Stowe. Sojourner Truth to Audre Lorde. Ida B. Wells-Barnett to Zora Neale Hurston. Frederick Douglass to Marcus Garvey. *Tarzan* to *Planet of the Apes*. Public Enemy to Queen Latifah. Langston Hughes to James Baldwin. Thomas Jefferson to William Lloyd Garrison. W. E. B. Du Bois to Angela Davis.

People tied to racist ideas. People tied to antiracist ideas.

And you, dear reader? Do you want to be a segregationist (a hater), an assimilationist (a coward), or an antiracist (someone who truly loves)? The choice is yours.

Just breathe in. Inhale. Hold it. Now exhale slowly:

NOW.

BUT I have to warn you:

Scrolling will never be enough.

Reposting will never be enough.

Hashtagging will never be enough.

Because hatred has a way of convincing us that half love is whole. What I mean by that is we—all of us—have to fight against performance and lean into participation. We have to be participants. Active. We must be players on the field, on the court, in our classrooms and communities, trying to *do* right. Because it takes a whole hand—both hands—to grab hold of hatred. Not just a texting thumb and a scrolling index finger.

But I have to warn you, again:

We can't attack a thing we don't know.

That's dangerous. And...foolish. It would be like trying to chop down a tree from the top. If we understand how the tree works, how the trunk and roots are where the power lies, and how gravity is on our side, we can attack it, each of us with small axes, and change the face of the forest.

So let's learn all there is to know about the tree of racism. The root. The fruit. The sap and trunk. The nests built over time, the changing leaves. That way, your generation can finally, actively chop it down.

TIMELINE
of Key Moments in American History

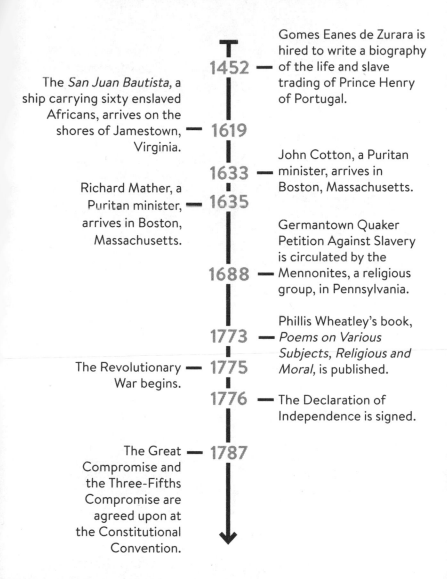

Gomes Eanes de Zurara is hired to write a biography of the life and slave trading of Prince Henry of Portugal.

1452

The *San Juan Bautista*, a ship carrying sixty enslaved Africans, arrives on the shores of Jamestown, Virginia.

1619

1633 John Cotton, a Puritan minister, arrives in Boston, Massachusetts.

Richard Mather, a Puritan minister, arrives in Boston, Massachusetts.

1635

Germantown Quaker Petition Against Slavery is circulated by the Mennonites, a religious group, in Pennsylvania.

1688

Phillis Wheatley's book, *Poems on Various Subjects, Religious and Moral,* is published.

1773

The Revolutionary War begins.

1775

1776 The Declaration of Independence is signed.

The Great Compromise and the Three-Fifths Compromise are agreed upon at the Constitutional Convention.

1787

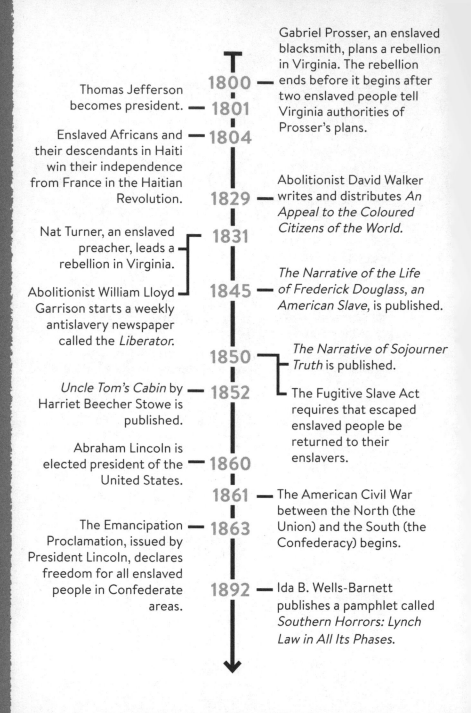

1800 — Gabriel Prosser, an enslaved blacksmith, plans a rebellion in Virginia. The rebellion ends before it begins after two enslaved people tell Virginia authorities of Prosser's plans.

Thomas Jefferson becomes president. — **1801**

Enslaved Africans and their descendants in Haiti win their independence from France in the Haitian Revolution. — **1804**

1829 — Abolitionist David Walker writes and distributes *An Appeal to the Coloured Citizens of the World*.

Nat Turner, an enslaved preacher, leads a rebellion in Virginia. — **1831**

Abolitionist William Lloyd Garrison starts a weekly antislavery newspaper called the *Liberator*. — **1845** — *The Narrative of the Life of Frederick Douglass, an American Slave,* is published.

1850 — *The Narrative of Sojourner Truth* is published.

Uncle Tom's Cabin by Harriet Beecher Stowe is published. — **1852** — The Fugitive Slave Act requires that escaped enslaved people be returned to their enslavers.

Abraham Lincoln is elected president of the United States. — **1860**

1861 — The American Civil War between the North (the Union) and the South (the Confederacy) begins.

The Emancipation Proclamation, issued by President Lincoln, declares freedom for all enslaved people in Confederate areas. — **1863**

1892 — Ida B. Wells-Barnett publishes a pamphlet called *Southern Horrors: Lynch Law in All Its Phases*.

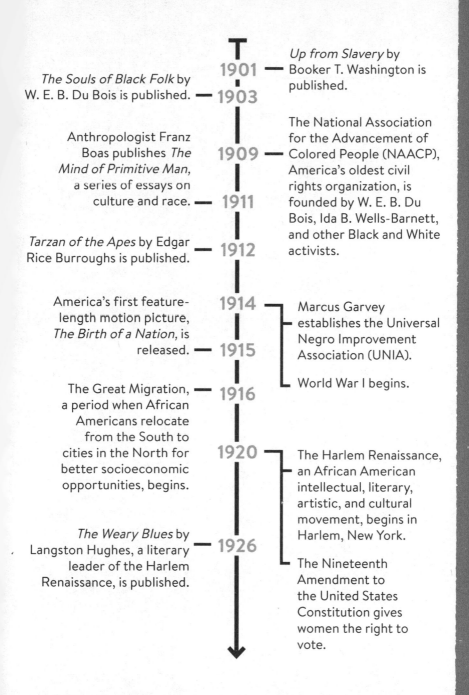

The Souls of Black Folk by W. E. B. Du Bois is published.

1901
1903

Up from Slavery by Booker T. Washington is published.

Anthropologist Franz Boas publishes *The Mind of Primitive Man,* a series of essays on culture and race.

1909
1911

The National Association for the Advancement of Colored People (NAACP), America's oldest civil rights organization, is founded by W. E. B. Du Bois, Ida B. Wells-Barnett, and other Black and White activists.

Tarzan of the Apes by Edgar Rice Burroughs is published.

1912

America's first feature-length motion picture, *The Birth of a Nation,* is released.

1914
1915

Marcus Garvey establishes the Universal Negro Improvement Association (UNIA).

World War I begins.

The Great Migration, a period when African Americans relocate from the South to cities in the North for better socioeconomic opportunities, begins.

1916

1920

The Harlem Renaissance, an African American intellectual, literary, artistic, and cultural movement, begins in Harlem, New York.

The Weary Blues by Langston Hughes, a literary leader of the Harlem Renaissance, is published.

1926

The Nineteenth Amendment to the United States Constitution gives women the right to vote.

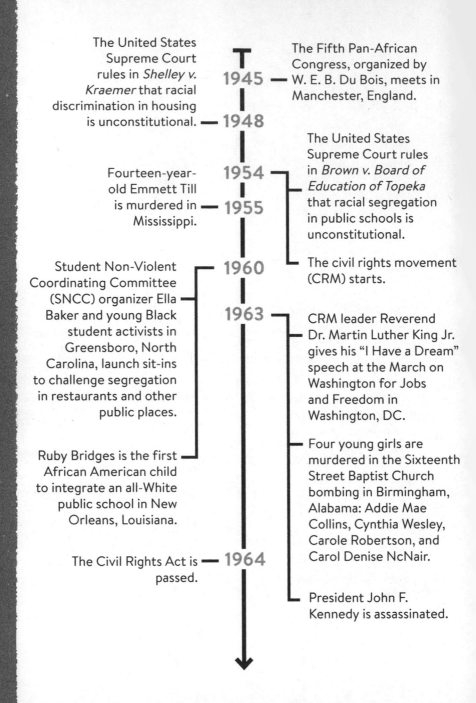

1945 — The Fifth Pan-African Congress, organized by W. E. B. Du Bois, meets in Manchester, England.

The United States Supreme Court rules in *Shelley v. Kraemer* that racial discrimination in housing is unconstitutional. — **1948**

Fourteen-year-old Emmett Till is murdered in Mississippi. — **1954** — The United States Supreme Court rules in *Brown v. Board of Education of Topeka* that racial segregation in public schools is unconstitutional.

1955

1960 — The civil rights movement (CRM) starts.

Student Non-Violent Coordinating Committee (SNCC) organizer Ella Baker and young Black student activists in Greensboro, North Carolina, launch sit-ins to challenge segregation in restaurants and other public places.

1963 — CRM leader Reverend Dr. Martin Luther King Jr. gives his "I Have a Dream" speech at the March on Washington for Jobs and Freedom in Washington, DC.

Four young girls are murdered in the Sixteenth Street Baptist Church bombing in Birmingham, Alabama: Addie Mae Collins, Cynthia Wesley, Carole Robertson, and Carol Denise NcNair.

Ruby Bridges is the first African American child to integrate an all-White public school in New Orleans, Louisiana.

The Civil Rights Act is passed. — **1964**

President John F. Kennedy is assassinated.

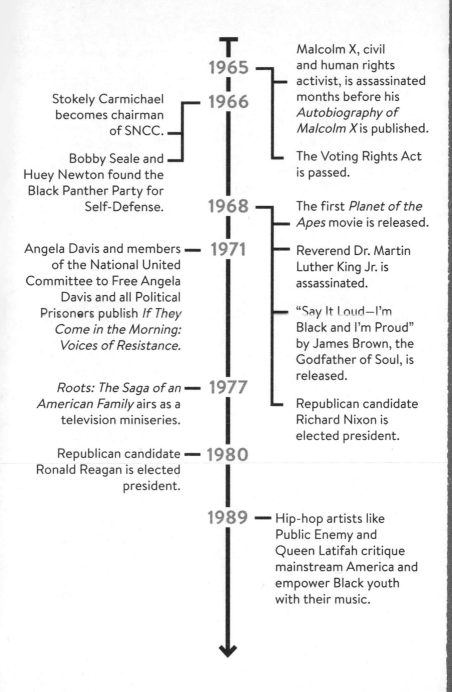

1965

Malcolm X, civil and human rights activist, is assassinated months before his *Autobiography of Malcolm X* is published.

1966

Stokely Carmichael becomes chairman of SNCC.

Bobby Seale and Huey Newton found the Black Panther Party for Self-Defense.

The Voting Rights Act is passed.

1968

The first *Planet of the Apes* movie is released.

1971

Angela Davis and members of the National United Committee to Free Angela Davis and all Political Prisoners publish *If They Come in the Morning: Voices of Resistance.*

Reverend Dr. Martin Luther King Jr. is assassinated.

"Say It Loud—I'm Black and I'm Proud" by James Brown, the Godfather of Soul, is released.

1977

Roots: The Saga of an American Family airs as a television miniseries.

Republican candidate Richard Nixon is elected president.

1980

Republican candidate Ronald Reagan is elected president.

1989

Hip-hop artists like Public Enemy and Queen Latifah critique mainstream America and empower Black youth with their music.

1992 The Los Angeles uprisings occur after police officer charged with brutally beating Rodney King are found not guilty.

Antiracist scholar and activist Angela Davis speaks about the importance of supporting Black women in academia at the "Black Women in the Academy: Defending Our Name, 1894–1994" conference.

1994 Democratic candidate Bill Clinton is elected president.

2000 Republican candidate George W. Bush is elected president.

United Nations World Conference against Racism, Racial Discrimination, Xenophobia and Related Intolerance takes place.

2001

2002 No Child Left Behind becomes law and expands state-mandated standardized testing.

September 11 attacks on the World Trade Center and the Pentagon. President Donald Trump later uses this attack as a justification for his executive order that prevented people from several Muslim countries from entering the United States.

2005 Hurricane Katrina devastates the poor, largely Black community in southern Louisiana. More than 1,800 people die.

2008 Democratic candidate Barack Obama is elected to become the first African American president.

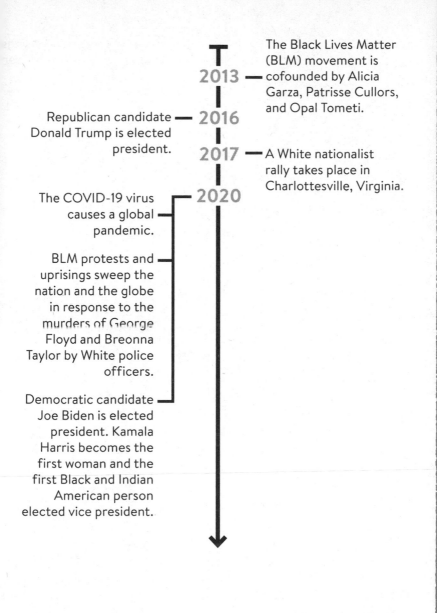

2013 — The Black Lives Matter (BLM) movement is cofounded by Alicia Garza, Patrisse Cullors, and Opal Tometi.

Republican candidate Donald Trump is elected president. — **2016**

2017 — A White nationalist rally takes place in Charlottesville, Virginia.

The COVID-19 virus causes a global pandemic. — **2020**

BLM protests and uprisings sweep the nation and the globe in response to the murders of George Floyd and Breonna Taylor by White police officers.

Democratic candidate Joe Biden is elected president. Kamala Harris becomes the first woman and the first Black and Indian American person elected vice president.

GLOSSARY

abolish (*uh-bol-ish*): To completely put an end to a system, practice, or institution

antiracist (*an-tee-rei-suhst*): One who expresses the idea that racial groups are equal and who supports policy that reduces racial inequity

assassinate (*uh-sas-uh-neyt*): To murder in a surprise attack for political or religious reasons

assimilationist (*uh-sim-uh-ley-shuh-nist*): One who expresses the racist idea that a racial group is culturally or behaviorally inferior, believing that a racial group can be changed for the better by acting like another racial group

blackface (*blak-feys*): Black makeup worn by White performers to exaggerate and mock Black people

citizen (*sit-uh-zuhn*): A legally recognized subject of a particular country, state, or commonwealth

colonialism (*kuh-loh-nee-uh-liz-uhm*): A country or region taking power and ruling over another country and its citizens

color-blind (*kuhl-er-blahynd*): The idea that someone "doesn't see" race and is therefore free from racial prejudice

colorism (*kuhl-uh-riz-uhm*): Prejudice or discrimination within a racial or ethnic group against individuals with darker skin in favor of those with lighter skin

contradiction (*kon-truh-dik-shuhn*): A situation in which statements or ideas are in opposition to one another

convert (*kon-vurt*): To change one's own beliefs or religious faith, or to force that change upon another

discrimination (*dih-skrim-uh-ney-shuhn*): Unjust or prejudicial treatment of people, based on factors of their identity

enslave (*en-sleyv*): To make someone a slave

equality (*ih-kwol-ih-tee*): A state of being equal, especially in status, rights, and opportunities

equity (*ek-wi-tee*): Justice, freedom from bias

feminist (*fem-uh-nist*): One who believes in the social, economic, and political equality of women and men

fugitive (*fyoo-ji-tiv*): A person who has escaped from a place or is in hiding to avoid arrest or punishment

ghetto (*get-oh*): A part of a city that is generally seen as undesirable and is occupied by a group or groups of people who have been negatively affected by social, legal, or economic conditions

humanity (*hyoo-man-i-tee*): Compassionate behavior toward all people

identity (*eye-den-ti-tee*): The characteristics that define who people are, the way they think about themselves, and how they are viewed by the world

immigration (*im-ih-grey-shuhn*): Moving from one country to another permanently

inequality (*in-ee-kwol-ih-tee*): Unequal distribution of resources and opportunities

inequity (*in-ek-wi-tee*): Lack of fairness and justice

inferior (*in-feer-ee-or*): Of less importance or value

inhuman (*in-hyoo-muhn*): Cruel; lacking human qualities of compassion, kindness, and mercy

injustice (*in-juhs-tis*): Unfairness

integrate (*in-ti-greyt*): To end the segregation of people in institutions and society by combining formerly separated groups

justice (*juss-tis*): Fairness based on the rules of law

law (*lah-w*): The system of rules that a particular country or community recognizes and enforces

liberation (*lib-uh-rey-shuhn*): Freedom from imprisonment, slavery, or oppression

lynch (*linch*): To execute, especially by hanging, without a legal trial

missionary (*mish-uh-nare-ee*): A person on a religious mission, often to promote Christianity, in another country

oppression (*uh-presh-uhn*): Continued cruel or unjust treatment or control

pandemic (*pan-dem-ik*): A widespread problem, especially a disease, that occurs over a large geographic area

policy (*pol-uh-see*): A principle or method of action proposed or followed by a government, business, or individual

politician (*pol-i-tish-uhn*): A person who is professionally involved in politics, such as a candidate for or holder of an elected office

postracial (*pohst-rey-shuhl*): Suggesting a period of time or a society where racial prejudice and discrimination no longer exist

privilege (*priv-lij*): An advantage, benefit, or immunity granted or available only to a particular person or group

protest (*proh-test*): A declaration or action in disapproval of or objection to something

race (*rayz*): An invented definition to categorize a group of people who share a particular physical trait, like skin color

racism (*ray-siz-uhm*): Prejudice or discrimination toward, or systemic oppression of, a person or people, based on their race or ethnicity, particularly one that is marginalized

racist (*ray-sist*): One who supports a racist policy through action or inaction or who expresses a racist idea

radical (*rad-i-kuhl*): Advocating for complete political or social change

refugee (*ref-yoo-jee*): A person who has been forced to leave their country in order to escape war, danger, or natural disaster

renaissance (*ren-uh-sahns*): A movement or period of intellectual and artistic growth

representation (*rep-ri-zen-tey-shuhn*): Speaking for or acting on behalf of someone; the description or portrayal of someone or something in a particular way

resist (*ri-zist*): To fight against the force or effect of something; to remain strong

revolt (*ri-vohlt*): To break away from or rise against a force or authority

savage (*sav-ij*): Untamed, wild; a brutal or vicious person

segregation (*seg-ri-gey-shuhn*): The discriminatory separation of groups of people based on race, ethnicity, or class

segregationist (*seg-ri-gey-shuh-nist*): One who expresses the idea that one racial group is permanently inferior and supports policy that keeps groups separate

self-reliance (*self-ri-lahy-uhns*): Utilizing one's own powers and resources rather than depending on those of others

slavery (*sley-vuh-ree*): The institution and practice of owning and treating human beings as property and forcing them into bondage

standardized (*stan-der-dahyzd*): Something that conforms to an idea set up by authority and used as a measure, norm, or criteria to evaluate

stereotype (*ster-ee-uh-tahyp*): A widely held judgment and oversimplified image or idea of a particular type of person or thing

supremacist (*suh-prem-uh-sist*): A person who believes that a particular group—especially one determined by race, religion, or sex—is better than all others and should therefore dominate society

supremacy (*suh-prem-uh-see*): Having ultimate authority, power, status, and dominance over others

unconstitutional (*uhn-kon-sti-too-shuh-nl*): An action that goes against the constitution or government of a country

FURTHER READING

ILLUSTRATED BOOKS

Antiracist Baby by Ibram X. Kendi, illustrated by Ashley Lukashevsky (Kokila, 2020)

Birmingham, 1963 by Carole Boston Weatherford (Wordsong, 2007)

The Book Itch: Freedom, Truth & Harlem's Greatest Bookstore by Vaunda Micheaux Nelson, illustrated by R. Gregory Christie (Carolrhoda Books, 2015)

Fifty Cents and a Dream: Young Booker T. Washington by Jabari Asim, illustrated by Bryan Collier (Little, Brown Books for Young Readers, 2012)

Heart and Soul: The Story of America and African Americans by Kadir Nelson (Balzer + Bray, 2011)

The Highest Tribute: Thurgood Marshall's Life, Leadership, and Legacy by Kekla Magoon, illustrated by Laura Freeman (Quill Tree Books, 2021)

I Have A Dream by Dr. Martin Luther King, Jr., illustrated by Kadir Nelson (Schwartz & Wade Books, 2012)

I've Seen the Promised Land: The Life of Dr. Martin Luther King, Jr. by Walter Dean Myers, illustrated by Leonard Jenkins (Amistad, 2004)

Show Way by Jacqueline Woodson, illustrated by Hudson Talbott (G. P. Putnam's Sons Books for Young Readers, 2005)

The Undefeated by Kwame Alexander, illustrated by Kadir Nelson (Versify, 2019)

Unspeakable: The Tulsa Race Massacre by Carole Boston Weatherford, illustrated by Floyd Cooper (Carolrhoda Books, 2021)

Woke: A Young Poet's Call to Justice by Mahogany L. Brown with Elizabeth Acevedo and Olivia Gatwood, illustrated by Theodore Taylor III, foreword by Jason Reynolds (Roaring Brook Press, 2020)

CHAPTER BOOKS

Black Heroes: 51 Inspiring People from Ancient Africa to Modern-Day U.S.A. by Arlisha Norwood (Rockridge Press, 2020)

Escape from Slavery: The Boyhood of Frederick Douglass in His Own Words, edited and illustrated by Michael McCurdy (Knopf Books for Young Readers, 1993)

Ruby Bridges Goes to School: My True Story by Ruby Bridges (Scholastic, 2009)

She Persisted: Harriet Tubman by Andrea Davis Pinkney (Philomel, 2021)

Who Was Sojourner Truth? by Yona Zeldis McDonough (Penguin Workshop, 2015)

OLDER READERS

Betty Before X by Ilyasah Shabazz with Renée Watson (Farrar, Straus and Giroux, 2018)

Brave. Black. First. 50+ African American Women Who Changed the World by Cheryl Hudson, illustrated by Erin K. Robinson (Crown, 2020)

Brown Girl Dreaming by Jacqueline Woodson (G. P. Putnam's Sons/Nancy Paulsen Books, 2014)

A Child's Introduction to African American History by Jabari Asim, illustrated by Lynn Gaines (Black Dog & Leventhal, 2018)

Finding Langston by Lesa Cline-Ransome (Holiday House, 2018)

Ghost Boys by Jewell Parker Rhodes (Little, Brown Books for Young Readers, 2018)

A Good Kind of Trouble by Lisa Moore Ramée (Balzer + Bray, 2019)

King and the Dragonflies by Kacen Callender (Scholastic Press, 2020)

Legacy: Women Poets of the Harlem Renaissance by Nikki Grimes (Bloomsbury Children's Books, 2021)

Loretta Little Looks Back: Three Voices Go Tell It by Andrea Davis Pinkney, illustrated by Brian Pinkney (Little, Brown Books for Young Readers, 2020)

March (Books 1–3) by John Lewis, with Andrew Aydin, illustrated by Nate Powell (Top Shelf Productions, 2016)

Mighty Justice: The Untold Story of Civil Rights Trailblazer Dovey Johnson Roundtree by Dovey Johnson Roundtree and Katie McCabe, adapted by Jabari Asim (Roaring Brook Press, 2020)

Miles Morales: Spider-Man by Jason Reynolds (Marvel Press, 2017)

New Kid by Jerry Craft (Quill Tree Books, 2019)

One Crazy Summer by Rita Williams-Garcia (Quill Tree Books, 2010)

One Last Word: Wisdom from the Harlem Renaissance by Nikki Grimes (Bloomsbury Children's Books, 2020)

The Only Black Girls in Town by Brandy Colbert (Little, Brown Books for Young Readers, 2020)

Roll of Thunder, Hear My Cry by Mildred D. Taylor (Puffin Books, 1976)

This Book Is Antiracist: 20 Lessons on How to Wake Up, Take Action, and Do the Work by Tiffany Jewell, illustrated by Aurélia Durand (Frances Lincoln Children's Books, 2020)

We Rise, We Resist, We Raise Our Voices edited by Wade Hudson and Cheryl Willis Hudson (Crown, 2018)

A Wreath for Emmett Till by Marilyn Nelson, illustrated by Philippe Lardy (Houghton Mifflin Harcourt Books for Young Readers, 2005)

ACKNOWLEDGMENTS

When I reflect upon the fullness of my life, the feeling that rises to the surface is gratitude. There is so much and so many I am thankful for.

I am deeply grateful to Jason Reynolds and Ibram X. Kendi for your brilliance and for inviting me to write this adaptation of *Stamped*. I am humbled by your trust in me to shepherd this work into the hands of younger readers. I am incredibly thankful for the team at Little, Brown Books for Young Readers for your support and guidance.

Frank, I'm so glad it was me you saw first on the steps of McEwen Hall. Thank you for your enduring love and belief in me. Imani, you are my greatest blessing. My village is wide and deep. Edward, Mary, Eddie, you are the pillars. Colleen Cruz, Carolyn Denton, Tricia Ebarvia, Shana Frazin, Amanda Hartman, Portia James, and Dana Johansen, you've been my anchors.

I want to especially thank three young early readers who provided precious feedback: Ella Cherry, Aidan H., and Dahlia Tomei. You live the wisdom of Audre Lorde's words: "It is not our differences that divide us. It is our inability to recognize, accept, and celebrate those differences." May you and all the children who read this book continue to lead the way.

—*Sonja Cherry-Paul*